The Phonics Handbook

THE PHONICS HANDBOOK

A Comprehensive Guide for Reading Teachers

MARY JO FRESCH

Routledge
Taylor & Francis Group
NEW YORK AND LONDON

A Stenhouse Book

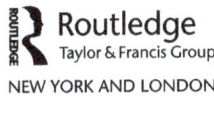

Designed cover image: Getty Images

First published 2026
by Routledge
605 Third Avenue, New York, NY 10158

and by Routledge
4 Park Square, Milton Park, Abingdon, Oxon, OX14 4RN

Routledge is an imprint of the Taylor & Francis Group, an informa business

© 2026 Mary Jo Fresch

The right of Mary Jo Fresch to be identified as author of this work has been asserted in accordance with sections 77 and 78 of the Copyright, Designs and Patents Act 1988.

All rights reserved. The purchase of this copyright material confers the right on the purchasing institution to photocopy pages which bear the copyright line at the bottom of the page. No other parts of this book may be reprinted or reproduced or utilised in any form or by any electronic, mechanical, or other means, now known or hereafter invented, including photocopying and recording, or in any information storage or retrieval system, without permission in writing from the publishers.

Trademark notice: Product or corporate names may be trademarks or registered trademarks, and are used only for identification and explanation without intent to infringe.

ISBN: 978-1-04102-401-9 (pbk)
ISBN: 978-1-00361-918-5 (ebk)

DOI: 10.4324/9781003619185

Typeset in Adobe Text Pro
by Apex CoVantage, LLC

Access the Support Material: www.routledge.com/9781041024019

To Hank
Who always has been, and still is, the wind beneath my wings

Contents

Acknowledgments — ix

Chapter 1 Learning About the English Language — 1
Developing a Command of English 2
The Code 3
Phonics Instruction 5
A Brief History of Phonics Instruction 6
Approaches for Teaching Phonics 7
What's Ahead 8
Chapter Summary 9

Chapter 2 Application Routines — 11
Routine 1: Build It 13
Routine 2: Find It 14
Routine 3: Sort It 15
Routine 4: Remember It 17
Routine 5: Match It 18
Routine 6: Unscramble It 20
Chapter Summary 21

Chapter 3 Consonants: Single Letters, Blends, Digraphs, and Silent Pairs — 23
The Consonant Sounds 24
Consonant Digraphs 32
The Consonant Blends 35
Silent Consonant Patterns 37
Application Routines in Action 38
Chapter Summary 40

Chapter 4 Vowels: Short, Long, *R*-Controlled, Diphthongs, Schwa, Digraphs — 41
Short Vowel Sounds 42
Long Vowel Sounds 44
R-Controlled Vowel Sounds 49
Diphthongs 51
Schwa 51

        Digraphs 52
        Application Routines in Action 53
        Chapter Summary 54

Chapter 5   Onsets and Rimes   57

        Why Rime Instruction Is Important 58
        The Thirty-Seven Rimes 59
        Resources for More Words 65
        Application Routines in Action 65
        Chapter Summary 66

Chapter 6   Syllables   69

        Why Do Syllables Matter? 69
        Teaching Syllables 70
        Types of Syllables 71
        Application Routines in Action 76
        Chapter Summary 78

Chapter 7   But Wait! There's More!   79

        But Wait! There's More on Structural Analysis 80
        But Wait! There's More on Homonyms 83
        But Wait! There's More on Word Origins 85
        But Wait! There's More on the Rest of the "nyms" 86
        Application Routines in Action 87
        Chapter Summary 88

Appendix A How Consonants Are Articulated   91
Appendix B Consonants   93
Appendix C Vowels   97
Appendix D Syllables   101
Appendix E Word Origins   103
Appendix F Application Routines   107
Bibliography   111
Index   115

Acknowledgments

I begin with humble thanks to Terry Thompson. You are the best editor and "thought partner" a writer could wish for. Your enthusiasm for this book from proposal to finished copy was a gift. To my brother, David Olivo, thanks for all the times you started my day with a phone call and a laugh. To our daughter Angela and son-in-law Nate, our son Mike and daughter-in-law Lori, thank you for being the behind-the-scenes cheerleaders. I'm thankful for our five amazing grandchildren – Nicholas, Vincent, Gavin, Christopher, and Avery – who readily share their love. You are evidence of how important it is to have teachers who provide the best possible instruction to make students lifelong, accomplished readers. Thanks to Violet for putting her early literacy skills to work. And finally, to my husband Hank, thanks for all your support and times you did double duty so I could sit and write. You are a great first draft reader, and your praise of the work I do is so appreciated. And to the readers of this book: thank you for bringing me into your teaching life. A book only has energy when it has readers – so thank you. Finally, I want to remind you of the important role you play in children's lives. Forty years after I finished teaching third grade, a former student found me through social media and shared that I was his favorite teacher. We truly never know how far our reach is – so thank you for all you do!

Chapter 1

Learning About the English Language

Tell me and I forget, teach me and I may remember, involve me and I learn.
– Benjamin Franklin (1706–1790)

I follow the line of first graders down the hall, on our way to music class. We are about to pass the kindergarten hall display, "The Leaves of Fall," when our line leader, Henry, throws his arms out and stops everyone's forward motion. He steps up to the display and slowly drags his finger across "The." Henry turns to me and yells, "THE!" This magic moment was no small victory. Henry had been sounding out the word *the* as /t/-/hē/ since the first week of school. I involved him in all sorts of ways to notice and think about the *th* digraph, but *the* stumped him over and over. My patience was critical in giving him the confidence to try one more time. Later that afternoon, he was reading aloud to me from his free-time book. As he worked across the text, slowly segmenting, then blending sounds, he came to *the*. I have to say, I held my breath . . . but Henry looked up at me, gave a sly sideways smile, and said *"THE."* High five, Henry, high five! This was a watershed event for him – suddenly, the letters he saw and the sounds they could make fell into place. The conversations that swirled around "his" word drew in other novice readers (every student in line that morning took their turn to point and read aloud *THE*). Our community of learners celebrated and supported each other as their phonics skills grew.

Finding ways to help our students actively develop the skills to be independent and fluent readers is the goal of all teachers, regardless of grade level. Primary teachers help young readers build foundational knowledge of connecting the sounds of English to the letters of the alphabet. Intermediate teachers look to the load of content vocabulary students must learn and how to best help them become users of these words for the long term. In both cases, the teacher's goal is to help students lift print from the page in efficient and accurate ways.

If you are a classroom teacher, knowing the fundamentals of phonics is critical, no matter what instructional program or approach you use. Not just our students need to know about phonics. As the educator driving the instructional planning, having a strong knowledge base *about* phonics puts you at an advantage. Our personal experiences with learning to read with phonics often guide our choices. But, if you did not learn phonics along the way . . . never fear! This book is intended to fill your toolbelt with knowledge about how English "works." That toolbelt needs pockets for consonants, vowels, syllables, onsets and rimes, and fascinating facts to engage students in not only learning phonics and vocabulary, but also to make sense of the English language. Besides strengthening your instructional choices, this knowledge gives you insights into assessing students who might be struggling in reading and/or writing. What *we* know helps us guide our students to become strong literacy users.

DEVELOPING A COMMAND OF ENGLISH

Poets and comedians enjoy poking fun at the English language. We have poems about how *dough* and *cough* don't rhyme and that *dead* rhymes with *bed* not *bead*. British comedian Michael McIntyre suggests "silent letter day" as he hilariously questions the *b* in *subtle* and *h* in *hour* (available on YouTube for a very big laugh). These examples all seem to show us what we often hear – English is so irregular! However, statistics help us understand the true facts about English (Moats 2000):

- 50% of our words are predictable sound-letter correspondences. These are words we can easily sound across, such as *hit, snap, cold*.
- 36% are predictable except for one sound (often the vowel). That one unpredictable sound may actually follow rules, such as the pattern where *a* is silent in *oa* (/ō/, *boat*), the *ea* sound can be /ā/ (*great*), *k* is always silent in *kn* (*knit*), and *w* is always silent in *wr* (*write*).
- 10% can be figured out if we know information such that words related in meaning are related in spelling and origin. For instance, we do not hear the *g* in *sign*, but do in *signature*; *leotard* doesn't appear to follow phonics rules, but it is an eponym (see Chapter 7 and Appendix E); and *chaos* doesn't have the more common /ch/ sound because it is a word of Greek origin, thus explaining the /k/ sound of *ch* (see Chapter 3).
- 4% of English words are true oddities. For example, *broad*, *eye*, and *two* somehow found their way into English. *Broad* is of unknown origin, so it remains a mystery why the *oa* has

Learning About the English Language

the /aw/ sound. *Eye* traces back to Old English *ege* meaning *eye*. How the pronunciation and spelling shifted is unknown. *Two* goes back to Proto-Indo-European (the "mother" of all languages) as *dwo*, making its way to Proto-Germanic as *twa*. When the spelling changed to *two* is unknown.

So, stay tuned! Much of what critics of the English language say will be resolved in the coming chapters. It gets down to knowing the "rules" that exist and how we can leverage that information when we read (decode) and write (encode). Did you notice . . . *code* is in both reading and writing? So, let's look at "the code."

THE CODE

We'll begin with some basics. First, a definition of *phonics*. Take a few seconds to think about what that word means to you. Phonics is knowing the sounds (*phonemes*) of the language and how the letters (*graphemes*) of the alphabet represent them. How do the sounds we hear map onto the letters? The English alphabet and the sounds they make are not a one-to-one match. Think of all the different sounds of the letter *a* in these words:

- *hat*
- *car*
- *make*
- *caution*
- *pizza*

What sound does *a* make? These examples give us five different spellings for the vowel sound of *a*. As you look at these words, hopefully, you are thinking: the sound of *a* depends on where it is in the word and what other letters are around it. Why is that? English has twenty-six letters but forty-four sounds. That means some letters make more than one sound, and some sounds are made by different letters or combinations of letters. Think of the words *cat* and *keep* – same sound at the beginning of the words (/k/) but written with different letters (*c, k*).

Just for Fun

When speaking about letters, we often refer to them as *uppercase* and *lowercase*. Do you know the origin of this? Before the printing press, handwritten letters were called *majuscule* ("slightly larger letter") or *minuscule* ("slightly smaller letter"). Once the printing press became popular, a way to sort the letters was needed. Printers sorted letters into trays, which they stored in cases – the larger letters in the *uppercase* and smaller letters in the *lowercase*.

Let's consider an official definition of phonics. According to the *Literacy Glossary*, published by the International Literacy Association (2024), *phonics* is:

> An approach to teaching reading that emphasizes the systematic relationship between the sounds of language and the graphemes (i.e., letters or letter combinations) that represent those sounds. Learners apply this knowledge to decode printed words. (unpaged)

Young learners need to learn this "systematic relationship." They first hear the sounds of our language so they can later connect those to the letters that represent them. Babies are born with the ability to hear every sound in every language. Over time, the sounds not used by the language or languages they hear drop out of their repertoire of what they attend to and imitate. This ability to hear the sounds, which young children must develop, is called *phonemic awareness*. A *phoneme* is the smallest unit of sound in language. It is all about what we hear. If you say /n/, /ī/, /t/, it could be *knight* or *night*. With either word, we hear three sounds (or, phonemes). If I'm just listening, the sounds don't tip me off to which spelling is meant – that's where context comes in. *Awareness* means the child *can* hear those three distinct sounds. This is an important step in reading development. Research shows a strong link between children's phonemic awareness and their later ability to learn to read. Researchers Monica Melby-Lervåg, Solvieg-Alma Lyster, and Charles Hulme (2012) were interested in the growing body of studies about "phonological awareness, phonological memory, and children's word reading skills" (322). After reviewing 235 studies, they found "the pivotal role of phonemic awareness" (322) as one of the strongest predictors of reading success.

Traditionally, the saying goes, "you can do phonemic awareness activities in the dark." That is, we only have to listen, not view. However, recent research advises going beyond oral-only phonemic awareness instruction. David Rehfeld, Marie Kirkpatrick, Nicole O'Guinn, and Rachel Renbarger (2022) used seven databases, finding 1,643 studies examining phonemic awareness instruction. Their meta-analysis narrowed to 138 studies that specifically documented findings for students with reading disabilities. They found students made greater gains in learning how to segment and blend words when they were presented with written letters and their sounds as part of phonemic awareness instruction. A meta-analysis by Florina Erbeli, Marianne Rice, Ying Xu, Megan Bishop, and J. Marc Goodrich (2024) also found oral-only phonemic awareness (PA) instruction inferior to instruction that included the visual connection of letters and their sounds. They suggest the importance "of early PA instruction in preschool through first-grade settings so that students acquire the PA and phonological-orthographic associations" (345), or the sound-letter correspondences. Studies such as these provide evidence that the Science of Reading continues to evolve and inform practice, demonstrating the need to incorporate visuals of letters and words during phonemic awareness experiences.

Now let's return to our discussion of "the code." The forty-four English sounds fall into two categories – consonants and vowels. We represent sounds with letters. Some sounds are represented

Learning About the English Language

by single letters – such as *s* (/s/) as in *send* – although it could also be represented by the letter *c* as in the word *cent*. Some sounds need two letters, such as *sh* or *ch*. Learning and retaining representation of sounds is called *orthographic mapping*. This mapping is important because once we retain sound and symbol relationships, our reading becomes more fluent. We automatically tap into this knowledge.

Educators need to understand sound and symbol relationships to help students regardless of the level taught. Knowing that *c* makes the /s/ sound before *e* is going to help me teach a first grader to read the word *cent*, and it is going to help me teach a fourth grader to read the word *cerebellum*. Although the words have different difficulty, the same sound and letter relationship applies (*c* = /s/ in *cent* and *cerebellum*). We will talk more about the specifics of all forty-four sounds throughout the following chapters.

PHONICS INSTRUCTION

Did you learn to read using phonics? Do you use phonics today when you come to a new word? If I ask you to read *electroencephalograph*, I'm guessing you will decode it by:

- noticing you can break it into syllables, beginning with *electro*
- knowing the *c* before *e* makes the /s/ sound
- being aware the *ph* in the middle and end of the word make the /f/ sound
- seeing the open syllable *lo* that makes *o* have the long vowel sound /ō/
- breaking the last syllable to the recognizable word *graph*

You probably did that in a few seconds as you sounded across the word using multiple phonics principles (and maybe thought . . . hey, no wonder they say EEG!). That type of quick decoding is what we hope our students can develop independence in, giving fluency to their reading.

A cautionary note about phonics is that it can only get you close to a word you have in your listening vocabulary. No matter how many times I try to sound out a word, if it does not click as a familiar word I have heard before, I may be unsure that I am sounding it out correctly. Phonics has two main aspects – the *segmenting*, or taking apart a word, and *blending*, or putting together those sounds. We use phonics when we encounter print and try to decode (read) the word. We look across the word, segmenting it into the sounds that correspond to the letters we see. We blend those sounds to arrive at the word we see. We also use phonics when we encode (write). We listen across the word, segmenting it into the sounds and deciding which letters correspond to the sounds we hear. Once we write the word, we blend the sounds to proofread and check to see if it looks correct. Time and experience speed up both processes.

> **Just for Fun**
>
> Executive functions are the mental processes that enable us to plan, focus attention, remember instructions, and successfully juggle multiple tasks. These functions play an important role in coordinating and bridging word recognition and language comprehension. Our brain is essentially the "air traffic controller" of learning and synchronizing new skills. A fun way to have students engage in executive functioning tasks is to create sorts using buttons. Ask students to sort and then explain why they put them together as they did. Colors? Shapes? Number of holes for the thread to pass through? Once they create a set of categories, have them share how they grouped the objects. Suggest students sort in a new way, using a suggestion from a classmate. The Application Routine, Sort It, is suggested in several of the chapters. Because our brains naturally look for patterns, having students look closely at similarities and differences with sets of words helps solidify their understandings about letter/sound relationships.

Phonics is not just about the sound of *a* but also prefixes, suffixes, and Greek and Latin roots we see in words. If you teach a content area, there are plenty of new words for students to read and learn. We can't teach the content if they can't read the vocabulary. So, whether you are a kindergarten teacher or a fourth-grade math teacher, a deep understanding of the language will help your students learn to read independently and fluently.

A BRIEF HISTORY OF PHONICS INSTRUCTION

In the United States, we have passed through several instructional methods since the late 1700s. In colonial times, the alphabetic approach focused on learning the alphabet, syllables, and memorization of biblical passages. In 1836, William McGuffey thought instruction should include stories that taught the alphabet and single-syllable words. He wrote some of these stories, testing them on his own children. One difference that stood out from other early reading texts like this was that McGuffey included illustrations. As the books were added for older grades, he included more difficult content and vocabulary. The books were used across the United States, selling more than 122 million copies by 1925.

However, the 20th century saw the arrival of the "look and say" whole word method in series such as *Fun with Dick and Jane* (Gray and Arbuthnot 1946). Less attention was paid to phonics in these books, as the stories were created using controlled, high-frequency vocabulary (e.g., *Oh, oh, oh. Look Jane. Look and see.*). In 1955, Rudolph Flesch challenged the whole word method and pressed for phonics instruction in *Why Johnny Can't Read and What You Can Do About It*. His publication was the first to encourage parents to take an interest in how their children were being taught to read. The debate between whole word or phonics continued. In 1967, Jeanne Chall published *Learning to Read: The Great Debate*, an inquiry into the methods being used from 1910 to 1965. Study results showed that teaching phonics was more effective than whole word. Following Chall's influential publication, many synthetic phonics programs appeared. These consisted of crafted stories that taught particular sound patterns (e.g., *The fat*

Learning About the English Language

cat sat on the mat.). Many educators felt these stories were stilted and did not utilize natural language.

In the 1980s, a grassroots movement, Whole Language, was spearheaded by classroom teachers. They believed using texts with natural language, such as children's picture books, would develop literacy skills. Researcher Ken Goodman (1986) claimed that "direct instruction in phonics is neither necessary nor desirable to produce readers" (215). However, over time, lack of organized scope and sequence of skills and less explicit instruction were major criticisms of this approach. In 1990, Marilyn Adams, a cognition specialist, suggested Whole Language methods shift to a focus on phonics, in her book *Beginning to Read: Thinking and Learning about Print*.

As the debate of how and if phonics should be instructed continued, at the request of the United States Congress, the National Institute of Child Health and Human Development, and the U.S. Department of Education assembled a panel of experts in 1997. They were charged with the task of examining research studies to find evidence of the most effective way to teach reading. Among other findings, the *Report of the National Reading Panel* (2000) concluded phonics instruction "makes a significant contribution to children's growth in reading" (2–132). The Science of Reading, or the decades of literacy research that inform our profession, confirmed that students need phonics to read and write with independence and fluency.

APPROACHES FOR TEACHING PHONICS

There are several ways to teach phonics. Let's define typical approaches so you can identify the type of instruction you might be required to use in your teaching. Some programs will combine the methods described as follows. No matter which approach you use, your personal knowledge of phonics is critical for facilitating the best instruction.

In **analogy** phonics, students are taught to attempt unfamiliar words by comparing them to a known word or word part. That is, they look for the part of an unfamiliar word that might be identical to a familiar word. A student sees the word *treat* and recognizes *eat* because they are familiar with the word *meat*. They know what those last three letters sound like (/ēt/) and then use that to sound out *treat*. This, of course, relies on previous experiences and an established sight vocabulary but does encourage use of phonograms (see Chapter 5) for the analogies.

With **analytic** phonics, students focus on larger units such as whole words to analyze the letter-sound relationships. Lessons use a whole-to-part approach. We might take a word like *meat* that students know and ask them to talk about what makes the /ēt/ sound (which is *ea* and *t* in this case). We'd then follow up by asking what other words they know with that sound and spelling pattern. As with analogy, students need to be able to read some words to get to this type of analysis, but it is explicit in instruction.

Embedded phonics is a more implicit level of teaching. In this approach, the teaching is incidental. For instance, I'm reading a poem to the students and say, "*pop* and *hop* rhyme. What part of those words makes them rhyme?" Then we would discuss /ŏp/ and try to think of other, similar words (*mop, top, chop, stop*). Sometimes when teachers are reading aloud, they have a teachable moment, so they take advantage of the time to discuss letter-sound connections. This puts the learning in real-world texts, but this approach often does not provide sequential or explicit skill development. Teachers need to keep good track of what they have taught while being aware of what students have mastered and what skills still need instruction.

Finally, **synthetic** phonics teaches students to explicitly convert letters to sounds and sounds to letters. Lessons uses a part-to-whole approach. We might spend an entire lesson on the /m/ sound. *Mmmmm – what starts with mmmm? Mary, marshmallow, monkey, money.* Time is spent teaching each sound until they can be built and blended into words. If we have learned /m/ and know /ŏ/, we can put them together to make /m/ . . . /ŏ/ . . . /m/ – mom! Special texts are often written to teach specific phonic elements. These texts provide experience in applying new sound-symbol relationships.

Regardless of the method you use, this book's intention is to support you in your teaching. Many teachers worry that too much skill and drill will kill (wow, listen to that *-ill* phonogram family!) the desire to read. We also worry about our students who struggle. How are they learning and applying their phonic knowledge? Not helping students develop the skills they need puts them at a long-term disadvantage regarding fluency and comprehension. Cognitive neuroscientist Mark Seidenberg makes the case that "poor readers have more difficulty decoding . . . [and] because their decoding skills are poor, they have to rely more on guessing words from context" (2017, 130). By not strengthening their phonics skills, students use inefficient strategies. Helping them develop their phonics knowledge is critical.

And what of the decodable books some students are given after instruction? Handing students texts they can read is empowering in ways we might not remember since it's been a long time since we first learned the code. Yes, it's not the great American novel, but this type of text can help build confidence, as students have opportunities to *apply* what they are learning. Such work solidifies new knowledge and builds confidence.

WHAT'S AHEAD

The next chapter gives six Application Routines to supplement your phonics instruction. These are designed to help students apply what they are learning. Regardless of the program you use, these routines will give students the opportunity to apply and extend their understanding of phonics rules you have taught. Keep these routines in mind as you read the subsequent chapters. Whenever you see an image of an Application Routine in action, you can find the accompanying documents available for download at MaryJoFresch.com and www.routledge.com/9781041024019. Use the Application Routines following your planned instruction to give students extra practice to assist in automaticity of making letter and sound connections. At the end of each chapter, three routines are showcased with specific descriptions of how to use them in your classroom.

You will also find some "Just for Fun" sidebars in each chapter. These describe engaging activities students can do to further apply their developing knowledge and, well, just have fun! Each chapter closes with recommendations for Further Reading. These professional articles support and extend the information in each chapter. They are ideal to use for deeper study or as conversation starters in professional development with other teachers.

The remaining chapters highlight specifics of English that are important to know. These support all phonics instruction, regardless of your instructional approach:

- Chapter 3 examines the reliability and dependability of the sounds of the twenty-five consonant letters. Single consonants, digraphs, blends, and silent patterns are explored, with examples provided.
- Chapter 4 explains the six vowel sound categories. Features of short and long vowels, *r*-controlled vowels, schwas, digraphs, and diphthongs illuminate rules and help us understand the nineteen vowel sounds of English.
- Chapter 5 presents the rationale and resources for including onsets and rimes during phonics instruction. These high-frequency phonograms offer power to students, as they can apply them to more than 500 primary words.
- Chapter 6 defines and gives examples of the six types of syllables. Knowing how to discern syllables helps in both reading and writing.
- Finally, Chapter 7 – But Wait! There's More! – reviews some important and often unexplored topics to build a more robust understanding of the way English works.

CHAPTER SUMMARY

We know phonics instruction gives our students a system for attacking words. The study of letter-sound correspondences provides independence in decoding (reading) and encoding (writing). Once students can hear the sounds of our language, they can connect them to the letter or letter combinations that represent the sound or sounds. Phonics instruction provides students with tools to unlock words when reading and writing. Whatever way a teacher or school district decides to help children learn to decode the language, systematic explicit instruction is crucial. Knowing how the English language works empowers teachers and helps their students learn independent strategies for reading and writing. In the next chapters, we will cover the forty-four sounds, along with some fun ways to engage students in learning.

So, let's fill your toolbelt!

Further Reading

Researcher Linnea Ehri examines how the Science of Reading informs our choices for teaching phonics:
Ehri, Linnea C. 2020. "The Science of Learning to Read Words: A Case for Systematic Phonics Instruction." *Reading Research Quarterly*, 55(1): 45–60.

Spelling is often taught as a memorization of words without consideration of how what we know about the English language helps us:
Joshi, R. Malatesha, Rebecca Treiman, Suzanne Carreker, and Louisa C. Moats. 2008. "How Words Cast Their Spell: Spelling Is an Integral Part of Learning the Language, Not a Matter of Memorization." *American Educator*, 6(16) (Winter 2008–09): 42.

A recent meta-analysis examined the importance of updating views on phonemic awareness instruction:
Erbeli, Florina, Marianne Rice, Ying Xu, Megan E. Bishop, and J. Marc Goodrich. 2024. "A Meta-Analysis on the Optimal Cumulative Dosage of Early Phonemic Awareness Instruction." *Scientific Studies of Reading*, 28(4): 345–370.

Chapter 2

Application Routines

. . . as one goes through life one learns that if you don't paddle your own canoe, you don't move.
— Katharine Hepburn (1907–2003)

Students benefit from practice that asks them to apply what they are learning in new and novel ways. Sarah Ash and Patti Clayton, educators interested in enhancing learning through application of new knowledge, suggest that "learning is maximized when it is active, engaged, and collaborative" (2009, 6). Learning something new, then demonstrating an understanding through application, is critical for independent use. Such practice also demonstrates who might need to circle back for additional instruction or support. This chapter describes six application routines that give learners practice with phonics principles you have already taught. When you use *Build It, Find It, Sort It, Remember It, Match It*, and *Unscramble It* you will be incorporating fun and engaging routines in your established curriculum. The phonics content for a routine is flexible and can be adjusted to meet your students' needs. Simply look at what you have already taught and use the suggestions below to craft a way for your students to apply what they are learning. You will be helping your community of learners practice their knowledge in a new way.

As a way to further support use of the routines, at the end of each of the following chapters specific examples of incorporating practice are provided. Applying what students have already learned encourages independence and facilitates orthographic mapping. Research shows that manipulation of letters and corresponding word work benefits students' encoding and decoding skills. Daniel Willingham is a psychologist who focuses on how cognitive science can inform K-12 education, particularly in terms of remembering what we are learning. He reminds us, "it is virtually impossible to become proficient at a mental task without extended practice" (2009, 107). These routines extend the phonics instruction you provide and gives students specific reasons to apply what they are learning.

Additionally, these routines build self-confidence and cognitive clarity about the concepts students are learning. Educators and researchers Patricia and James Cunningham state, "cognitive clarity is knowing what you are trying to do and understanding where you are trying to go and why you are going there. When you have cognitive clarity about a task, you are more likely to persist in your efforts because you anticipate the goals you will eventually reach" (2002, 88). These routines help develop cognitive clarity connected to instruction you have already provided. Once students know the routine, they can immediately become engaged in the required work, regardless of content. They will have intention to complete the learning task and understand that the content connects to ongoing phonics instruction.

When first introducing the routines, keep in mind that teacher modeling and think-alouds are key elements for success. Each routine should be explained and demonstrated to the whole group *before* students are asked to complete them on their own. This approach utilizes the gradual release of responsibility model that David Pearson and Margaret Gallagher found useful in their 1983 research. The stages of instruction ensure that students know what the expectations are as they move to independence. We begin with "first me" to show our learners how we think about and approach the task. By verbalizing our process, we make visible to students what we are thinking about as we complete the required work. We then invite the class to assist as "next we" do the work together. Here we collaborate and fine tune how to complete the task. Students gain a clear understanding of expectations. Finally, "now you" has learners working independently. We have scaffolded the process, and students can work on their own. Over time the learners can immediately become engaged in the routines, as they will have built independence through familiarity. They will know the demands of the routine and understand that the content changes throughout the year. This saves you time as the students have instant access to practicing and applying what they are learning in your phonics instruction.

The routines are applicable for side practice (learning centers, workstations, independent work) and small or large group work. Here, each routine is described, followed by examples of the routine in action, how it might be incorporated into various instructional structures, and ways to differentiate it for student needs. For quick reference, a chart summarizing these routines is available in Appendix F.

Application Routines

ROUTINE 1: BUILD IT

Students are given a phonic pattern and additional letters. They are asked to "build" as many words as they can. In this routine, students demonstrate their understanding of mapping sounds to letters and blending across words. Educator Patricia Cunningham, a strong supporter of phonics instruction, suggests giving students ways to have hands-on experiences. She notes that, through building words, learners discover making "small changes, such as changing just one letter or moving the letters around, result in completely new words" (2009, 112).

Example of the Routine in Action

Give students an index card or letter tiles showing *ay* along with additional, individual letters such as *b, d, h, j, l, m, p, r, s, w, cl, gr, pl, st, tr* (the number will depend on the amount of time your plans allow). Students are to construct and write down as many words as they can.

Using the Routine as Side Work

Place the letter cards where students have easy access. Include paper and pencils so they can record the words constructed. Provide an instruction sheet that informs students of the focus of their word building (in this case, *ay* words). Their work can be evaluated to ensure that students are creating real words.

Using the Routine in Small Group

Gather learners with similar needs around a table, placing the letter cards where they can view them. Ask if they see any words that can be made by adding the other letters to the phonic pattern. If the group needs more guidance, you might ask, "what word would I have if I added _____ to _____?" Buddies can be given a set of letters and the focus pattern to work together to create their list of words. Ask individuals to assist in writing the words so everyone in the group can see, using chart paper or whiteboard.

Using the Routine in Large Group

Gather students together in the whole group area. Display large versions of the letter cards where everyone can see them. Ask students if they see any words that can be made by adding the other letters to the phonic pattern. If the group needs more guidance, you might ask, "what word would I have if I added _____ to _____?" Ask volunteers to assist in writing the words on a large chart paper or whiteboard display.

Differentiating the Routine

Give individuals who need more experience with the pattern fewer additional letters and only letters that will make words. For those who are confident with the pattern, extend this routine by giving them additional letters that will not make real words. This will help you observe their ability to discern between letters that are useful and those that are not (in this case giving them letters such as *e, f, t, bl, tw*). More challenging letter combinations can be included (in this case *spr, str, sw*).

ROUTINE 2: FIND IT

Students are given texts they can independently read for targeted searches of words with specific phonic elements. You can find texts online or use a text they are currently using – such as selections from their free reading. This is also a great way to double up by using content texts. In this routine, students demonstrate their knowledge of letter/sound relationships by hunting for words with specific phonic patterns. Reading Rockets, a family-friendly website that posts research-based strategies suggests, "word hunts are a fun and engaging word study activity that encourages students to apply their knowledge of spelling patterns, sight words, or vocabulary words using classroom texts" (2025, unpaged) and helps learners make connections across words.

Example of the Routine in Action

Ask students to use their personal free reading text to search for words with the digraphs *sh* and *ch* (reminding or asking them about the sounds those two digraphs make – *sh* =/sh/, *ch* = /ch/, /sh/, /k/). As they find the words, they record them on a collection sheet.

Using the Routine in Small Group

Gather students with similar needs around a table and distribute a text you know they will be confident reading. You can slip printed texts inside sleeve protectors so they can use erasable markers to circle words. Ask readers to look at the text and see if they can find the target phonic element – *sh* and *ch* (this gives them time to preview and skim the article). You can ask group members to work with a buddy to find the targeted words. Or ask students to independently circle the words, giving you an easy "in the moment" assessment. Collectively make a list of the words found and review how they show the targeted phonic element(s). Ask group members if they know any other words with the targeted phonic element.

Using the Routine in Large Group

Gather the class together where you typically meet for whole group lessons. Project a text on a whiteboard or use an enlarged text that everyone can see. Ask the group to look at the text and see

Application Routines

if they can find the target phonic element – *sh* and *ch* (this gives them time to preview and skim the article). Collectively make a list of the words found and review how they show the targeted phonic element(s). Ask students if they know any other words with the targeted phonic element.

Differentiating the Routine

Give individuals who need more experience with the pattern a text that they can confidently read at 90–100% accuracy. Provide visual support by writing the phonic pattern (*sh* and *ch*) on an index card for them to use to compare to the text to find the words. For learners who are confident with the pattern, provide a more challenging text. After they have found the words with the pattern, ask them to think of related words for each (for instance, they find *chemical*, adding words such as *chemistry, chemist, chemically*). This gives an additional assessment of their vocabulary.

ROUTINE 3: SORT IT

Students are given a list of words to sort according to phonic patterns. The purpose of word sorting is to identify common patterns by creating categories of words that are similar. The sort is accomplished by comparing and contrasting the words. This can be offered as an open sort – where students establish (and justify) their own categories – or a closed sort where they are given key words to guide them as they compare and contrast. Modeling both types of sorts is critical for helping students understand what the task requires. Twelve word cards is a useful number to use, as it provides enough words for analysis but is not overwhelming. After establishing the categories, a generalization ("I/we sorted the words and discovered . . .") should be written about the words, so the students have "cognitive clarity" about the similarities and differences. The generalization, if created by the students on their own, provides insights into how they are analyzing and organizing the words. This may point to the need for additional instruction or suggest that the students might need the key words to point them in the right direction.

Example of the Routine in Action

Give students word cards to sort with the following written on them, one word per card – *dancing, jumping, stepping, swimming, hoping, asking, dropping, helping, skipping, making, matching, cutting*. Depending on the group's needs, provide key words (*hugging, talking, baking*) to help narrow the sort. Point out the differences in the key words. Or, if no key words are provided, after they have sorted, have students record their categories on a collection sheet. Ask them to

write a generalization about their findings ("I sorted my words and discovered . . ."). This allows assessment of how they are analyzing the words.

Using the Routine as Side Work

If using as an open sort, provide the twelve targeted word cards and paper for the students to record their categories. Once they create their categories, they are to write a generalization about it (such as, in the example, "I sorted my words and discovered there are three ways *-ing* is added to base words – if the word ends in *e* it is dropped and *-ing* is added, if the word has a short vowel the consonant is doubled before adding the suffix, other words simply have the suffix added"). If using as a closed sort, provide the twelve targeted word cards and paper with key words (such as *hugging, talking, baking*) for the students to sort and record their categories. In either case, after establishing the categories, a generalization should be written about the words, so the students have "cognitive clarity" about the similarities and differences that can be applied beyond the twelve words sorted.

Using the Routine in Small Group

Gather a group of students with similar needs around a table and lay out word cards with the following written on them (one word per card) – for example, *dancing, jumping, stepping, swimming, hoping, asking, dropping, helping, skipping, making, matching, cutting*. Ask students to read the words to themselves, then take turns reading them aloud. Ask what they notice about all the words. Guide them to focus on the suffix at the end of the word. Do they see that all words end in *-ing*? What else do they notice (guide them to see that some words have letters doubled, some drop the *e,* and others simply have the *-ing* added to them). Establish three key words (e.g. *hugging, talking, baking*) and ask students to help sort the twelve words into the three categories. Together develop a generalization about how *-ing* is added to words, so the students have "cognitive clarity" about the similarities and differences ("We sorted our words and discovered there are three ways *-ing* is added to base words . . ."). Invite the group to think of other words that might fit into any of the three categories.

Using the Routine in Large Group

Gather the group together where you typically meet for whole group lessons. Display word cards with the following written on them, one word per card – for example, *dancing, jumping, stepping, swimming, hoping, asking, dropping, helping, skipping, making, matching, cutting*. Distribute cards to "buddies" and ask them to read the word to themselves. Have buddies read their word aloud. Ask the group what they notice about all the words. Guide them to focus on the way *-ing* is added to the base word. Ask the students to help sort the twelve words into the three categories. Together develop a generalization about the words, so the students have "cognitive clarity" about the similarities and differences ("We sorted our words and discovered there are three ways *-ing* is

Application Routines

added to base words . . ."). Ask students if they can think of other words that might fit into any of the three categories. Write these on index cards and add to the listings. Invite them during the week to add any words they come across in their reading that fit into the categories.

Differentiating the Routine

Give individuals who need more experience with the pattern words they can easily read, or you can read aloud to them (for example, *seeing, loving, being, cooking, changing, dining, naming, feeling, living, shopping*). Use fewer words (ten in this case) and show the key words (*hugging, talking, baking*). Ask the students to listen to and look at the word you read aloud – which key word does it look like? Do they know any other words they can add to the list? For students who are confident, provide more challenging words to sort (e.g., *exaggerating, establishing, illuminating, decreasing, conflicting, securing, detecting, shredding, fulfilling, equipping, differing, remembering*). You can also do this without key words, asking students to create their own. Ask them to develop a generalization about the words, to justify their categories and to demonstrate their understanding of the similarities and differences. They should then add other words they know to demonstrate their understanding of the categories.

ROUTINE 4: REMEMBER IT

Students are given a set of cards to match. To play this memory game, place cards face down and turn over two at a time to try to make matches, reading the card aloud as they work. If their cards do not match, they turn them back over for the next student to try. Psychologists Timothy Brady, Talia Konkle, George Alvarez, and Aude Oliva study issues regarding visual long-term memory capacity. In their 2008 study, they found a task that required looking at and then trying to deliberately remember objects provided promising results for memory. They found being clear in explaining the requirement to look and remember triggered better long-term memory. This routine requires focus on word details to remember the location of matching words.

Example of the Routine in Action

Create two copies of six word cards: *face, prey, bay, bait, sleigh, break*. The twelve cards are turned face down and students take turns trying to match the word cards, reading aloud the card drawn. If the cards do not match, they turn them back over and the next student takes their turn.

Using the Routine as Side Work

Place the twelve cards where students can work independently. They should spread out the cards, face down. They turn over two at a time to try and match, reading the cards aloud as they turn them face up. They can play as a small group or individually. Ask students to take one or more of the words and think of another word with the same phonic pattern (*face – pace, prey – they*) and record that on a collection list that can be left out for other students to add to and for you to assess.

Using the Routine in Small Group

Gather students with similar needs around a table, placing the twelve cards where they can take turns flipping two cards to make a match, reading each word aloud as they draw a card. Ask each student to take one of the words cards and think of another word with the same phonic pattern (e.g., *face – pace, prey – they*).

Using the Routine in Large Group

Gather the group together where you typically meet for whole group lessons, placing the twelve cards where everyone can take turns flipping two cards to make a match, reading each word aloud as it is drawn. Ask the group to look at the words and think of another word with the same phonic pattern (e.g., *face – pace, prey – they*). Make a list of these on chart paper or another display that can be kept up for several days. Invite students to add to the list whenever they find similar words while they are reading.

Differentiating the Routine

For individuals who need more support, position half of the cards face up and half face down. Ask them to then try to make their matches, reading each card aloud as they draw. Alternatively, the sets of word cards can be written on two different colors of paper. Students know to choose one of each color to try to make a match, therefore increasing the chances for success. To challenge students, choose more difficult patterns (/aw/ words *awkward, authority*, /oi/ words *voice, ploy*) to read aloud and ask them to create a list of words with similar patterns.

ROUTINE 5: MATCH IT

Students match word cards to phonic sound cards (for example, *bay* matches to /ā/, *time* matches to /ī/). By studying the words, students sound them out and begin to retain them as sight words. Linea Ehri, an expert on reading development, stresses the importance of systematic phonics instruction. Making connections with sounds and letters is critical to orthographic mapping, which, she tells us, "occurs when, in the course of reading specific words, readers form connections between written units, either single graphemes or larger spelling patterns, and spoken units, either phonemes, syllables or morphemes" (2014, 5). This routine focuses on having students make sound and letter connections.

Application Routines

Example of the Routine in Action

Give students six word cards with specific phonic elements (for example, *bay, time, bone, map, milk, shop*) and six cards with those phonic sounds (/ā/, /ī/, /ō/, /ă/, /ĭ/, /ŏ/). The cards are sorted matching the word card to the phonic sound card.

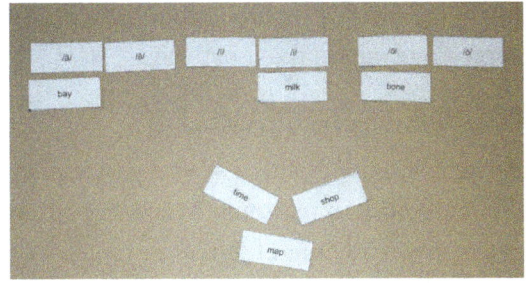

Using the Routine as Side Work

Place the six word cards and six phonic sound cards where students have access. Explain that they are to match the word to the correct sound card and to record the matches they made on paper (for later assessment). Ask them to then add other words to their record sheet that they know with the same phonic sounds.

Using the Routine in Small Group

Gather students with similar needs around a table. Place the six word cards and six phonic sound cards face up, where the students can see them. Explain that they are to match the word to the correct sound card. Work as a small group, reading aloud the word card, then searching for which phonic sound card matches. Ask the students for other words that have the same phonic sound and record those on a chart or display.

Using the Routine in Large Group

Gather the group together where you typically meet for whole group lessons. Place the six word cards and six phonic sound cards where everyone can see them. Explain that they are to match the word to the correct sound card. Work as a group, reading aloud the word card, then searching for which phonic sound card matches. Ask the group for other words that have the same phonic sound. Write these on a chart or other display that can be available during the week. Invite students to add to the list as they find similar patterned words in their reading materials. At the end of the week, gather the group together and review the words added to the chart. Discuss how the phonic sound might have been found in words related to the ones used during the activity or interesting multisyllabic words.

Differentiating the Routine

For individuals who need more support, have fewer phonic sound cards and more word cards that match (*bay, cage* – /ā/, *teen, me* – /ē/, *bone, coat* – /ō/) or choose words they can match to pictures that identify the vowel sound (*cake* – /ā/, *tray* – /ā/, *snow* -/ō/, *smile* – /ī/, *dog* /ŏ/, *truck* – /ŭ/). To challenge students, give them more difficult words to match to the phonic sound card (*though* – /ō/, *sweat* – /ĕ/, *sleigh* – /ā/, *tough* – /ŭ/, *stamp* – /ă/, *scheme* – /ē/) or give these students cards with phonic sounds (e.g., /ō/, /ē/) and ask them to generate a list of words they know that contain those patterns.

ROUTINE 6: UNSCRAMBLE IT

Words containing phonic sound patterns students know are cut apart and the letters scrambled. Students work to reassemble each word from the list. This routine reinforces memory of patterns and visual matching of letters in target words. It also encourages sounding across the words to match phonic patterns.

Example of the Routine in Action

Give students a list of words (*crowd, owl, toy, oily, noun, coin, brown, spoil, shout, point*) that have been cut apart into individual consonants (*c, r, d, l, t, l, y, n, n, c, n, b, r, w, n, s, p, l, s, h, t, p, n, t*) and multiple copies of the phonic sound patterns on cards (*ow, oy, oi, ou*). Students are asked to study the list and choose the necessary letters to unscramble the word.

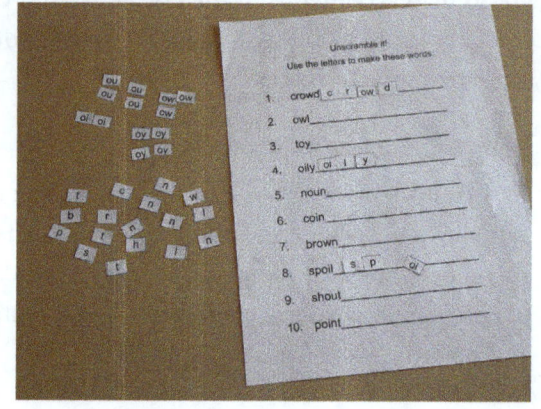

Using the Routine as Side Work

Provide the list of words (*crowd, owl, toy, oily, noun, coin, brown, spoil, shout, point*) that have been cut apart, using individual consonants (*c, r, d, l, t, l, y, n, n, c, n, b, r, w, n, s, p, l, s, h, t, p, n, t*) and multiple copies of the phonic sound patterns on cards (*ow, oy, oi*, etc.). Provide instructions that asks students to study the word list and use the individual letters to reassemble the words.

Using the Routine in Small Group

Gather individuals with similar needs around a table. Show them a list of words (*crowd, owl, toy, oily, noun, coin, brown, spoil, shout, point*), the individual consonants (*c, r, d, l, t, l, y, n, n, c, n, b, r, w, n, s, p, l, s, h, t, p, n, t*), and multiple copies of the phonic sound patterns on cards (*ow, oy, oi, ou*). Ask them to work together to reassemble the letters to create the words on the list. Ask the students if they know any other words with the sound patterns (*ow, oy, oi, ou*).

Using the Routine in Large Group

Gather the group together where you typically meet for whole group lessons. Show everyone the list of words (*crowd, owl, toy, oily, noun, coin, brown, spoil, shout, point*). Distribute to the entire group of learners the individual consonants (*c, r, d, l, t, l, y, n, n, c, n, b, r, w, n, s, p, l, s, h, t, p, n, t*) and multiple copies of the phonic sound patterns on cards (*ow, oy, oi, ou*). Show a word on the board or chart and ask students to examine what they have that might be part of that word (for

Application Routines

instance, *crowd* is displayed. Ask, "who has the vowel sound pattern in *crowd*? Please bring it to the front of the room. Now, who has the consonants that will help us in spelling *crowd*?") Continue to work together to reassemble the words on the list. Invite the group to add other words they know with the same sound patterns (*ow, oy, oi, ou*).

Differentiating the Routine

For individuals who need more support, use fewer words and keep the consonant digraphs/blends together to reduce the number of letters needed to reassemble the words (*cr, br, wn, sp, sh, nt*). To challenge students, use the same patterns that appear in multisyllabic words (*boisterous, moisture, outrageous, lounger, browsing*).

CHAPTER SUMMARY

In this chapter, six application routines were presented. These routines allow students to practice and apply what they are learning in their phonics instruction. Each routine is designed for a variety of uses in the classroom – side practice (learning centers, workstations, independent work) and small or large group work. Once students understand the demands of the routine, content can be changed, and they can quickly get to work applying their latest phonics instruction. In this way, new knowledge is solidified, and students gain confidence in applying what they are learning. We help them build independence and, as Katharine Hepburn says, "paddle their own canoe."

Further Reading

Patricia and James Cunningham provide a broad view of how to teach phonics and what our students need to be successful:
Cunningham, Patricia M., and James W. Cunningham. 2002. "What We Know About How to Teach Phonics." In *What Research Has to Say About Reading Instruction* (3rd ed.), edited by Alan E. Farstrup and S. Jay Samuels, 87–109. Newark, DE. International Literacy Association.

Students can show us how they are thinking about the phonic patterns they see. For an interesting view of one student's focus during word sorting:
Fresch, Mary Jo. 2000. "What We Learned from Josh: Sorting Out Word Sorting." *Language Arts, 77*(2) (January): 232–240.

A classroom teacher and a literacy researcher questioned the memorization model often used in weekly spelling instruction. Together, they created a plan that utilized word sorting:
Fresch, Mary Jo, and Aileen Wheaton. 1997. "Sort, Search, and Discover: Spelling in the Child-centered Classroom." *The Reading Teacher, 51*(1): 20–31.

Chapter 3

Consonants: Single Letters, Blends, Digraphs, and Silent Pairs

My father told me once that words and letters hold all the secrets of the universe.
– Eliza in *Bee Season* (Fox Searchlight Pictures 2005)

In this chapter we explore facts about consonants, consonant blends, consonant digraphs, and silent consonant pairs. Let's begin with baseline information about the consonant letters (graphemes) and sounds (phonemes).

- Twenty-one of the twenty-six letters in the English alphabet are consonants
- These twenty-one letters make twenty-five distinct sounds
- Eighteen consonant sounds are made by single letters
- Seven consonant sounds are made by digraphs (*di* meaning *two*, *graph* meaning *to write* – we write two letters to make a digraph)

We look first at consonant sounds, because these letters make fewer different sounds than the vowels. Recall that there are forty-four sounds in English. If twenty-five of these are consonant sounds, that leaves quite a few vowel sounds (nineteen!) for just a few letters (*a, e, i, o, u,* and sometimes *y*).

THE CONSONANT SOUNDS

To begin, let's examine the single consonant sounds. Beginning readers often find learning the sounds of the consonants easiest because they make fewer different sounds. Consonants are very useful when we are reading. They can help us as we sound across a word since many consonants have single, reliable sounds.

Fill in the spaces with the correct consonants for this sentence that has only vowels:

_e_'_ _ea_ _ _o_ _o_a_ _ _ou_ _ _!

Could you figure it out? Unlikely! Let's take out those vowels and fill in the consonants. Now try finishing the same sentence by filling in the vowels:

L_t's l_ _rn c_ns_n_nt s_ _nds!

(Answer: Let's learn consonant sounds!)

Was that a bit easier? Consonants are indeed important to us as a reader and writer! *Most* single consonants make one sound. What letters are the consonants? Saying all the letters that are not vowels is a good start. But what differentiates a consonant from a vowel? Say the vowels out loud – /aaaa/, /eeeeee/, /iiiii/, /oooooo/, /uuuuuu/ . . . notice what your mouth did? Was it open the entire time you pronounced the sound? Try this . . ./b-b-b-b/. Notice with *b* your lips came together. Try saying the sound for the letter *t* . . . /t-t-t-t/. That time your tongue went against the roof of your mouth. Now try *e* again . . ./e-e-e-e/. . . nothing is blocked when you say this sound. **Consonants are the sounds we make when we block the flow of air in some way.** It might be with our lips, teeth, tongue, roof of the mouth (or palate) or vocal cords. The vowels are unblocked . . . so the difference in consonant sounds from vowel sounds is whether or not we block air flow as we say the sound.

The consonant sounds represented by single letters are:

/b/ - boy	/k/ - kick/can	/s/ - son/cent
/d/ - dig	/l/ - lamb	/t/ - tap
/f/ - fish	/m/ - man	/v/ - van
/g/ - goat	/n/ - no	/w/ - wall
/h/ - hat	/p/ - pan	/y/ - yes
/j/ - jump/giant	/r/ - run	/z/ - zoo

Consonants

That is eighteen consonant sounds. An interesting part of these eighteen sounds is you can pair ten sounds that are voiced and unvoiced. Voiced consonants are those that make your vocal cords vibrate. Your vocal cords wrap around your air pipe. Say these two words out loud: *sip* and *zip*. Now say each one as you hold your fingers lightly against your throat. *Sip, zip*. With *zip* you can feel the cords vibrate, with *sip* we do not feel the vibration. This vibration is why we call some consonants voiced.

Voiced Consonant	Unvoiced Consonant
b	p
d	t
g	k
v	f
z	s

Some of these differences are easy to hear, such as the *z* and *s*. The primary reason we need to understand this is when students are writing and trying to sound out words they sometimes confuse the voiced and unvoiced sounds. If you know this, you can easily read their predicted spellings. It might also tip you off to a hearing or speech issue if they consistently confuse these sounds. We will talk about voiced and unvoiced sounds in other situations (such as all vowels are voiced) . . . so remember voiced = vibration, unvoiced = no vibration.

Anticipated Misunderstanding

In the early stages of literacy development, when students attempt to sound out and write words, they may write only consonants. That is due to the reliability of the sounds and how they are able to articulate them. For instance, a student might write *fvrt* for *favorite*. Once they become familiar with vowel sounds and their role in English words students will gradually begin to add these to their attempted spellings.

Let's practice some of these voiced and unvoiced consonant sounds . . . hold your hand against your throat and see if you feel vibration of your vocal cords (or not) as you say these word pairs out loud:

Voiced Initial Consonant	Unvoiced Initial Consonant
bat	pat
dent	tent
gill	kill
van	fan
zip	sip

For a handy chart that summarizes the following information on how consonants are classified by articulation, see Appendix A. This information is often used by phonics programs that include a sound wall. The sound wall shows each of the forty-four sounds by displaying photos or drawings of how the mouth positions change for each pronunciation. This tangible resource provides support as students learn to map the sounds of English onto the alphabet. Create your own sound wall at the link provided.

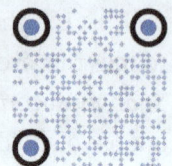

Consonants are also classified by *how* we say (or articulate) them:

1. **Plosives (also called stops) – the air flow is blocked as the sound is made, followed by a puff of air.** The location of air block in our mouth for these letters can be the lips (*b, p*), behind the teeth (*d, t*), and back of the throat (*g, k*). As you say *baby, pup, dog, tan, gate* and *kick* out loud, feel the puff of air from your mouth for the consonant sounds /b/, /p/, /d/, /t/, /g/, and /k/.

2. **Fricatives – the sound made by forcing a continuous stream of air through a narrow space.** The narrow space is created by placing the teeth on the lip (*f, v*), the tongue between the teeth (*th – voiced and unvoiced*), at the ridge behind the teeth (*s, z*), and on the roof of the mouth (/sh/, /zh/). Say *fan, vine, thin (unvoiced), they (voiced), sun, zoo, shark,* and *pleasure* out loud and pay attention to how your mouth changes and feel for the stream of air as you create the sounds /f/, /v/, /th/, /th/, /sh/, /zh/.

3. **Affricates – the sound that is a combination plosive (stop) and fricative.** The sounds are created by stopping the air flow and then immediately releasing it. As you say *jump* and *chain* notice this combination for the /j/ sound and the /ch/ sound. This also occurs when having the /j/ sound in words such as *gem, giant, cage,* and *dodge*. We also hear the /ch/ in *match*.

4. **Nasals – the sound made by closing the mouth and forcing the air through the nose.** This occurs by closing the lips (*m*), using the ridge behind the teeth (*n*), and using the back of the throat (*ng/nk*). Say *nose, mom, sing,* and *wink* out loud and feel the shift to the back of your throat as you say /m/, /n/, /ng/, and /nk/.

5. **Liquids – formed by slightly interrupting the airflow with no friction.** These include *l* and *r*. Louisa Cook Moats, a recognized expert in how children learn to read, especially those with learning challenges, notes these sounds are often "the most difficult to teach in speech therapy because they 'float' in the mouth. The liquids have no clear beginning or end point in articulation" (2001, 31). Say *lap* and *rat* out loud and pay attention to the slight interruption of air flow.

Consonants

6. **Glides – these sounds glide right into the vowel that follows it.** These occur on the roof of the mouth (*y*), the back of the throat (*wh*, /hw/), and in the throat (*h*). Say *yak, who, what*, and *hat* out loud and feel how the sounds glide right into the vowel sound.

Anticipated Misunderstanding

Consider the different ways the consonant sounds are pronounced. While we may not notice some of the subtle differences as a reader, it impacts a student's pronunciation. This influences how others understand what is being said and how a student sounds out their spelling attempts. If children are not differentiating enough between sounds as they sound out a word, such as with *p* and *b*, this will appear in their writing and offer you a teachable moment.

Not all the consonants are learned at the same rate or speed. The plosive sounds (/p/, /b/, /t/, /d/) are typically learned earlier than the fricative sounds (/f/, /v/, /s/, /z/). Of course, individual students will learn at different rates. Our takeaway from examining the differing articulations is helping students orthographically map the letters they see with the possible sounds they could make, and in turn, which letters could possibly make the sounds they hear. We also use this articulation information if our phonics instruction includes a sound wall. Our own care in how words are accurately pronounced as students listen is important for modeling.

Look back at the list of single consonant sounds on page 24. What consonant letters are missing? Did you notice there is no *c, q,* and *x* in the chart? Why is that? All three letters have no distinctive sound of their own.

C does not have a singular sound, rather, it has "hard" and "soft" sounds. The "hard" sound, represented in the previous list by *k*, is made when *c* is followed by the vowel letters of *a, o,* or *u* (*cat, coat, cup*). The other sound of *c*, represented in the list by *s*, occurs when it is followed by *e, i,* or *y* (*center, city, cyclone*). The hard and soft sounds of *c* have broader applications. If students know that *c* always softens to /s/ when followed by *e, i,* or *y*, then we must put *k* at the end of a word to "protect" the *c* when adding endings such as -ing, -ed, and -y. For example, *picnic* becomes *picnicking, panic* is *panicked*, and *mimic* is *mimicked*. The softening influence of the vowels that follow *c* is also seen when adding -able. The *e* at the end of the word is not dropped, again, to "protect" the soft sound of *c*. For example, *notice* is spelled *noticeable*, *service* is *serviceable*, and *trace* is *traceable*.

Anticipated Misunderstanding

It is not unusual for young leaners to predict spellings using the sound they are most familiar with, such as writing *kat* for *cat*. This provides a teaching opportunity. Ask students to look at the word they wrote. A good self-discovery tool is to tell students to use their B.E.E. – B(rain), E(ars), E(yes). Yes, your brain told your ears, this is what it sounds like, but our eyes see it as a reader and discover that doesn't look quite right. While we hear /k/, does that look right? Have they seen that word in print? What do they think might need to be changed to spell it conventionally?

Q alone does not have a distinctive sound. In English *q* is always followed by *u*, unless it is a loan word from another language (*Iraq, burqa, qigong*). The sound represented by *qu* sounds like /kw/. Most of the words come from Old English and were, in that time period, spelled *cw* (*quick* was *cwik*). Anglo-Saxon scribes first used *u* with *q*, but later returned to *cw*. With the influence of the Normans, *qu* became the standard for English spellings. While we will examine syllables in Chapter 6, we can note here that the number of vowel *sounds* we hear (not *vowel letters* we see) helps us count the number of syllables. However, as reading specialist Denise Eide reminds us, when written as *qu*, *u* "is not a vowel but part of a multi-letter phonogram" (2012, 81). For example, *quit* is one syllable (as we only hear the /ĭ/ vowel sound).

Just for Fun

Offer students a riddle . . . the word QWERTY does not follow the *qu* pattern. Why is that? QWERTY is the first six keys on the top row of a keyboard. American inventor Christopher Latham Sholes created the QWERTY layout of typewriter keys in 1874. Before that the keys were placed in alphabetical order. Often used letter pairs next to each other, such as *s* and *t*, created jamming problems. By separating the keys, typists could type much faster!

X also does not have a distinctive sound. In some words, the *x* sounds like /ks/ in the stressed syllable (*fox, exile, waxy*) and /gs/ in unstressed syllables (*exist, executive*). Rarely, a word begins with *x* but if it does the sound is /z/ (*xylophone, Xerox*).

Let's return to the chart of consonants with single sounds on page 24. What do we know about each that can inform our instruction? How consistent are the consonant sounds? At the end of the 1940s Paul Hanna directed a study that analyzed consistency and frequency of sounds in the English language. At that time schools introduced a new way of teaching spelling using sound-to-letter technique. It became apparent in his study that the consistent sounds were learned first by young learners. As his research continued, Hanna wondered exactly what the match was between sounds and letters in the words students would encounter in their elementary curriculum. Working in 1966 with Jean Hanna, Richard Hodges, and Edwin Rudorf, Paul Hanna analyzed over 17,000 most frequently used single and multisyllabic words, using the Thorndike-Lorge *Teacher's Word Book of 30,000 Words* as a guide for occurrence. Edward Thorndike and Irving Lorge's 1944 list was well known. The two researchers surveyed textbooks, juvenile books, the Bible, and magazines to create word lists, giving an occurrence of each word per million words. That is, how often did the word occur in print? Their list became a reference for spelling instruction for many years. Using the Thorndike-Lorge list, Hanna, Hanna, Hodges, and Rudorf collected their own list of 17,000 words and analyzed the consistency in letter/sound relationships. What was the reliability of teaching particular

Consonants

correspondences? They wanted instruction that would help students understand the structure of English, beginning with the most dependable sounds. This boosts our confidence in teaching these sounds and helps students build a solid foundation to independently sound out words as they decode and encode.

The consonants are presented in alphabetical order for handy reference, each with a few examples. The consonants and their dependability (along with examples) are also summarized in Appendix B.

1. B
    - is a consistent /b/ sound at the beginning of words (*back, beg, bike, boat, bus*)
    - can be silent when it follows *m* (*comb*) or precedes *t* (*debt*). In Old English *b* was pronounced in words such as *comb*, but over time it became silent (most likely because our lips go together to make *m* and *b*, so the *b* sound got lost) but the spelling remained the same. *Debt* is an example where the scribes wanted to honor the origin of the word, *debitum*, which was Latin . . . even though it had been spelled *dette* until then. In this case, the spelling changed, but the pronunciation did not.

> **Just for Fun**
>
> The origins of words, as well as pronunciation and spelling changes over time, can be found at eytmonline.com. Knowing we don't have all the answers about words, we can be comfortable saying to our students, "You know, I don't know why that word is spelled that way. Let's look it up." We empower students to investigate word origins and stories. We help them make memories about these unusual words, rather than just memorize them!

2. D
    - is a consistent /d/ sound (*day, den, dish, dog, dump*)
    - is said once if there are two together, as in *odd*

3. F
    - is a consistent /f/ sound (*fan, fed, fin, fold, fun*)
    - is said once if there are two together, as in *stuff*

4. G
    - 70% of *g* words have the more common hard sound (/guh/) when followed by *a, o,* or *u* (*gate, goat, gush*)

- 29% of *g* words make the soft sound (/j/) when followed by *e*, *i*, and *y* (*gentle, giant, gyroscope*)
- the remaining 1% *g* is silent when it precedes *n* (*gnaw, gnome, sign, design*)

5. H
    - is 99% consistent as the /h/ sound (*hat, hello, hit, hog, hug*)
    - is never the final sound in a word. It may be the final letter (*yeah, hurrah, Pooh*) but it is always silent
    - can be silent at the beginning of a word (in borrowed French words *honor, herb, hour, heir*)
    - can be silent when following *g* or *r* (*ghost, ghoul, rhyme, rhapsody*)

6. J
    - is a consistent /j/ sound at the beginning of a word (*jam, jet, jig, joke, just*)
    - like *h*, this letter never represents a sound at the end of a word. The sound /j/ can be heard at the end of words (*judge, huge*), but it is not represented by *j*

7. K
    - is a 99.5% consistent /k/ sound (*kale, keep, kind, kooky, kudo*)
    - is silent .5% of the time when it is followed by the letter *n* (*knack, knee, knit, know, knuckle*)
    - this letter is often confused with *c*, as it does the work of that letter in words like *car* and *cat*. Letter *c* sounds like /k/ 76% of the time.

8. L
    - is a consistent /l/ sound at the beginning of words (*last, let, like, long, lump*)
    - is silent before final *k* after *a* and *o* (*talk, chalk, yolk*) . . . but pronounced before final *k* following *i* (*milk, silk, milky*).

9. M
    - is consistent in the /m/ sound (*man, met, mice, mom, mud*)
    - reliable, as there is no other sound assigned to this letter

10. N
    - is a consistent /n/ sound (*name, new, nine, nose, nut*)
    - reliable, as there is no other sound assigned to this letter

Consonants

- can be silent when following *m* (*autumn, hymn*)
- *n* takes on a slightly different sound when it is followed by *g* and *k*. Say the words *note, ring,* and *sink*. Can you feel the slight shift in where the /n/ is sounded in each of these words?

11. P
    - is consistent in the /p/ sound (*page, pet, pin, pop, put*)
    - if it is written with *h* (*ph*) it makes the same sound as the letter *f*

12. R
    - is very consistent in the /r/ sound (*ray, rest, rib, rose, run*)
    - reliable, as there is no other sound assigned to this letter
    - can influence the vowel sounds it follows – *ar, er, ir, or, ur* (see Chapter 4)

13. S
    - 84% of the time *s* represents the unvoiced sound /s/ (*sand, sell, sip, soap, suds*)
    - 12% of the time it can represent the voiced /zh/ sound as in *treasure* and the /sh/ sound as in *sugar*
    - The /z/ sound is common for *s* at the end of a word when it is a plural. Say these words aloud . . . *jobs, birds, legs, hills* – do you notice that the words end in the consonant sounds that are voiced (*b, d, g, l*)? Now say *roofs, cups, cats* and you will see these words end in the unvoiced consonants (*f, p, t*) to make the /s/ sound

14. T
    - represents the /t/ sound 98% of the time (*tale, tell, tip, took, tub*)
    - is silent if it follows *f* or *s* (*often, soften, softener, hasten, fasten, listen, castle*)
    - if there are two together (*mitt, mutt, boycott*), we say the sound once, as we did the /d/ in *odd* and /f/ in *stuff*

15. V
    - is 100% consistent in the /v/ sound (*van, vest, vine, vote, vulture*)
    - has no other sound associated with it
    - no English word ends in the letter *v*

> **Just for Fun**
>
> The story of words that at one time ended in *v* and then had *e* added to them goes back to the scribes. At the time *u* and *v* looked very similar in handwritten manuscripts. Linguist David Crystal shares that the scribes "decided to add a final *e*, which they thought would help show that the *v* is a consonant" (2012, 62). They were not bothered by the idea that *e* was used to mark vowels long in some words (*make, ride*) – they were more concerned by the look of the written word. Thus, we have a number of words with a short vowel that also have the *e* marker – whose function is to eliminate any English words from ending in *v*. A fun reminder for students when they write words with short vowel sounds that end in *v* (*love, have, glove, move, give*) is the *e* is needed to "hold" the *v* up so it doesn't fall over! Remember, this is not an exception to the *e marker* rule, rather it is a rule about not having English words end in *v*.

16. W
    - consistent /w/ sound when a single consonant at the beginning of a word, followed by a vowel (*wave, went, wind, won*)
    - represents a vowel sound when the second letter in a vowel team with *a*, *e*, or *o* (*claw, flew, snow*). The *vowel+w* teams may end a word, unlike the similar sounding patterns /au/ (*saucer*), /eu/ (*neutral*), and /ou/ (*count*).
    - when *w* precedes *r* it is 100% predictably silent (*wrong, write, wrap*)

17. Y
    - is a consistent /y/ sound at the beginning of a word or syllable, when it functions as a consonant (*yam, yet, yip, you, yule, can-yon, be-yond*)
    - has three vowel sounds – long and short i (*cry, reply, satisfy, myth, gym, symbol*) and long e (*baby, candy, quickly, baggy*).

CONSONANT DIGRAPHS

There are seven consonant digraphs. Reviewing the definition of the word *digraph* we see *di* means *two* and *graph* means *to write*. We write two letters to make a digraph. However, those two letters do not maintain their individual sounds, but rather take on a new, unique sound.

1. /th/
    - is the most frequently occurring consonant digraph
    - can be voiced and unvoiced
        - *thick, thing, third, thaw* are examples of the unvoiced /th/, which occurs more frequently than voiced

Consonants

- *that, their, this, those* are examples of voiced /th/ (say those words aloud and feel the vibration on your throat)
  - A pattern to voiced and unvoiced *th* is a bit difficult to detect, but we do know that when *th* is preceded by a consonant it makes the unvoiced sound 100% of the time. Say the words *month*, *depth*, and *birth* for examples of this.

2. /sh/
   - second most occurring consonant digraph (*shall, sheep, shine, show, shut*)
   - is consistent and reliable in sound

3. /ch/
   - third most frequently occurring consonant digraph
   - 89% of the time it says /ch/ as in *chair, check, chin, chose, church*
   - 10% of the time it says /k/ as in *chaos, chemist, orchid, echo*
   - 1% of the time it says /sh/ as in *charades, chef, machine, brochure*
   - One more thing about /ch/ . . . sometimes it is written as *tch* as the end of a word . . . as in *match* and *ditch*. Notice that the vowel sound is short in these words. When the vowel sound is long, as in *peach* and *coach*, /ch/ is written as *ch* at the end of the word. So, the vowel sound influences how /ch/ is spelled at the end of words. This pattern applies 100% of the time.

Just for Fun

Why three sounds of *ch*? We hear the most common sound of *ch* in words like *church, chin, lunch, bleach*. These are Old or Middle English words. Words like *chaos, chemistry, chrome, echo,* and *scheme* are Greek in origin and have the /k/ sound. Words like *chef, charades, chateau,* and *brochure* are French in origin and have the /sh/ sound. When students come across a word containing *ch* the Old/Middle English sound (/ch/) is most likely but teaching them that two other languages can influence the sound shows them the reasoning behind the other sounds. They are not exceptions to the rule for the sound of *ch*, they are part of the history of that sound in English.

4. /ng/ and /nk/
   - *ng* is the next most frequently occurring consonant digraph
   - 100% consistency at the end of a word (*bang, ring, along, flung*)
   - never appears at the beginning of a word
   - You will notice in *change* the /ng/ sound seems to be different. So how can it be 100% of the time? Remember the influence of *e* and *i* on *g* that makes the soft sound of /j/? That

applies here as well. *Change, changing, challenge, challenging* are good examples of how *e* and *i* are very important to the sound of /ng/.

- The /ng/ sound also blends with the *k* in the /nk/ sound at the end of words like *sink*. Try saying these words – *sing, sink* . . . feel the difference in your throat? Although the spelling is *nk*, the *n* before *k* makes the /ng/ sound at the end of the word. This works 100% of the time you see *nk* . . . say *think, monkey, bank, Thanksgiving* . . . and you will hear (and feel) the sound.

5. *wh* /hw/
   - 90% of the time represents the /hw/ sound at the beginning of *wheel, where, whiskers*
   - /hw/ sound is never at the end of a word
   - The remaining 10% of the words have the /wh/ sound as in *what, where, when, why* – where the *h* is silent and we hear the /w/ sound. Did you notice the difference in your lips to say these?
   - American English has started to lose this differentiation . . . but in some parts of the country local dialects make them very different

6. *ph* /f/
   - consistent at beginning, medial, and final sounds of words (*phone, photo, phrase; nephew, alphabet, geography; graph, lymph, paragraph*)
   - less occurring in early literacy words

7. *gh* /f/
   - admittedly, this digraph has different pronunciations at the end of a few words due to word origins and "The Great Vowel Shift" (a two-century period in the history of English where speakers changed how they said the vowels but did not change the spellings)
   - combined with *au* in two base words and related words (*draught, draughts, laugh, laughing, laughter*)
   - when combined with *ou*, this digraph can be pronounced in two ways
     - Combined with short /o/ sound – "off" (*cough, trough*)
     - Combined with short /u/ sound – "uff" (*tough, rough, enough*)
   - this digraph will also be discussed in Silent Consonant Pairs because in some variations the *gh* is silent (*bought, thought, though, dough, through, bough*).

Consonants

The Consonant Diagraph is one of the most frequently used phonic elements in English and they are mostly predictable in their sounds. When seen together, the two letters take on a completely different sound than they do individually. Learning these helps students begin to decode across words with more proficiency, adding fluency to their reading.

THE CONSONANT BLENDS

Next, let's look at twenty-one frequently used two-letter and three-letter consonant blends. **Consonant blends are two or three consonant letters that retain their individual sounds as we blend them together.** Once students have learned the single consonant sounds described previously, blends can be taught. We use the dependable sounds of the single consonants and then blend them together. Say these sounds aloud . . . . /s/-/t/-/r/-/a/-/p/. Now blend them . . . . *strap*. You say and blend all three of the consonants at the beginning of the word. Let's say aloud a few more examples of words with blends. Try these, listening for the sounds of individual consonant sounds as you blend them together:

/s/-/t/-/o/-/p/

/p/-/r/-/a/-/y/

/s/-/n/-/a/-/p/

/s/-/c/-/r/-/u/-/b/

/s/-/p/-/l/-/a/-/t/

Think about the two or three consonant sounds you blended to say the word. Did you notice they retained their individual sounds? When we see them in print, they are often called Consonant Clusters, but when we sound them out, they are called Consonant Blends. They are highly dependable since they are composed of the reliable consonant sounds. The blends are best taught after students have had practice sounding out the single consonants, so they can carry that knowledge forward as they blend across two or three consonants that appear together.

Some time ago (1964) Edward Fry did an analysis of the most useful phonic sounds to teach. He recognized the problem many curriculum developers and teachers had in choosing what to teach first when it comes to phonics. One area he examined was the commonly occurring beginning consonant blends, according to frequency. Fry suggested teaching these twenty-one consonant blends in this order, due to their "high degree of consistency" (1964, 762):

Group 1: *st, pr, tr, gr, br*

Group 2: *pl, sp, cr, cl, dr, fr*

Group 3: *sc, bl, fl, sk, sl, sw*

Group 4: *sm, gl, sn, tw*

Fry goes on to say, we might also note that with the exception of *tw*, all the initial blends fall into only three families:

S family: *st, sp, sc, sk, sl, sw, sn,* and *sm*

R family: *pr, tr, gr, br, cr, dr,* and *fr*

L family: *pl, cl, bl, fl,* and *gl*

Teaching the blends in families might be helpful. (763)

> ### Anticipated Misunderstandings
> Learners sometimes let their ears dominate their spelling attempts. We've talked before about "predicted spellings" as they are writing using their current operating knowledge of the language. Common errors we often see are *jriv* for *drive* and *chrap* for *trap*. Say each of these words aloud, slowly. Do you hear the /j/ sound at the beginning of *drive*? How about the /ch/ sound at the beginning of *trap*? Ask students to use their B.E.E. to go back and look at what they wrote. As a reader . . . does that word look right? Could a real word start with *jr*? When helping students edit their work, suggest they use their B.E.E. first – and then see what type of help they might need from you or a peer.

Additionally, there are several common three-letter consonant blends:

thr (the digraph /th/ plus the consonant /r/ blended together; *three, throw, thread*)

shr (the digraph /sh/ plus the consonant /r/ blended together; *shred, shrug, shrink*)

spr, spl, squ, str, scr (each with its consistent sounds: *spring, splash, squish, street, scratch*)

Consonant blends are also found at the end of words. A few, like *sk, sp,* and *st* can be found at the beginning (*skate, sky, skid; spin, spot, spell; star, story, strong*) and end of words (*desk, risk, ask; wasp, asp, lisp; best, crust, fist*). Other ending consonant blends are:

ct	ft	ld	lf	lp	lt
duct	aloft	child	gulf	gulp	exalt
eject	craft	cold	itself	help	felt
fact	draft	field	myself	kelp	gilt
sect	raft	gild	shelf	scalp	kilt
pact	swift	wild	wolf	yelp	welt

Consonants

mp	nd	nk	nt	pt	rd
bump	blend	blank	cent	apt	award
camp	brand	drank	hint	crept	bird
lamp	kind	shrink	hunt	kept	guard
lump	pond	sink	paint	tempt	hard
ump	pound	stink	punt	wept	word

SILENT CONSONANT PATTERNS

We finish this chapter with twelve silent consonant patterns. David Crystal helps us understand a bit more about these silent consonant letter/sound correspondences. He notes that silent letters "have an etymological explanation. In some cases, an extra letter has been added to show a classical origin, as we saw in words like *debt*" (2012, 166). These silent letters have several highly regular functions. For instance, when saying *match*, we do not hear the *t* – the end of the word sounds like /ch/. This pattern (*tch*) with a silent consonant always follows a short vowel (*catch, fetch, pitch, notch, crutch*).

As Crystal suggests, exploring etymologies, or origins of words, can often explain to students how we arrived at the spellings we have. And we see that words related in meaning are related in spelling and the silent patterns are illuminated. For instance, *sign* contains the *gn* pattern (/n/), but we hear the silent letter in the related words *signature, signal, signify*, and *insignia*. We hear the silent letter *b* in *bombard, limber*, and *crumble*, which are related to the words with the *mb* pattern (/m/) in *bomb, limb*, and *crumb*.

We surveyed these silent patterns when we considered the single consonant sounds, but let's review and take a special look. Sample words are provided for each pattern to provide an idea of what you might use with any of the Application Routines in Chapter 2. The most frequent patterns are:

1. *tch* /ch/ – *match, fetch, itch, botch, hutch* (always follows a short vowel)

2. *dg* /j/ – *badge, edge, ridge, lodge, fudge*

3. *wr* /r/ – *wrap, wreck, write, wrong, wrung*

4. *kn* /n/ – *knack, knew, knit, know, knuckle*

5. *gn* /n/ – *assign, design, sign, cologne, gnaw, gnome*

6. *mb* /m/ – *lamb, climb, limb, tomb, thumb, crumb*

7. *lk* /k/ – *talk, chalk, stalk, yolk* (*l* is silent after *a* and *o*, but pronounced after *i* – *milk, silk, milky*)

8. *ps /s/ – psalm, psychology, psychic*

9. *wh /h/ – who, whose, whole, whom* (there are only a few words where the *wh* takes on the /h/ sound – more commonly it is the /w/ sound as in *what, when, white, whisker*)

10. *bt /t/ – debt, doubt, subtle*

11. *gh /g/ – ghost, ghastly, ghouls, spaghetti*
    - the letters *gh* are both silent in the *ight* pattern and will be discussed as one of the dependable long vowel sounds for *i* (*light, night, fright*)
    - the letters *gh* are both silent with other vowel combinations (*straight, daughter, eight, sleigh, neighbor, bought, thought, though, dough, bough*)

12. *mn /m/ – autumn, hymn, column, solemn*

APPLICATION ROUTINES IN ACTION

Now that we have examined the consonant sounds, here are three Application Routines students can engage in for more practice. You will want to adjust to your population, perhaps choosing different patterns or words, but this will get you started in planning for using the Routines following consonant instruction.

Application Routine Showcase: Find It with the Soft Sound of *g*

Invite students to hunt for examples of the soft sound of *g*. Ask students to use a book they are independently reading (these offer vocabulary that is accessible to each reader). Using books such as these differentiates the task simply by choosing texts they can independently read. Give them a copy of the following collection chart along with the directions:

Use your free reading book to hunt for words with the "soft sound of g" pattern. Remember that the soft sound of g sounds like /j/. The patterns to look for today are ge or gi. When you find a word, write it in the correct column. Be ready to share your findings!

Soft sound of g (/j/) spelled ge (as in gene)	Soft sound of g /j/ spelled gi (as in giant)

Hunting for and studying words helps solidify students' knowledge of these patterns. Sometimes our learners will look for the pattern, writing a word even if it does not meet the criteria. For instance, in this hunt they might find *get* or *give*. In this case, ask them to read these aloud – do they have the /j/ sound?

Consonants

Application Routine Showcase: Remember It with the Sounds of *ch*

Create two each of the descriptions of the three *ch* sounds on yellow paper squares: *ch that sounds like /ch/ as in chain, ch that sounds like /k/ as in chaos,* and *ch that sounds like /sh/ as in chef.* Write words with the three sounds of *ch* on white paper squares: *chop, chair, choir, echo, chute, machine.* Place the sound cards and word cards face down on a table. Have students take turns choosing a white card, reading the word, then choosing a yellow card to try to match the pattern. For example,

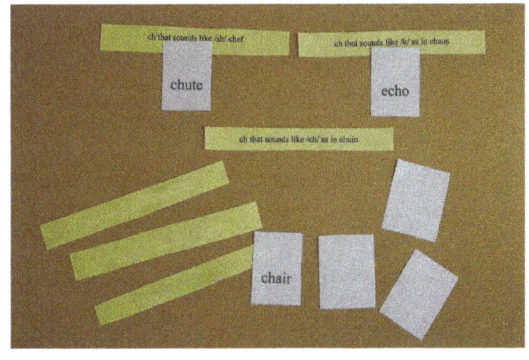

a student reads the word *chair*. They must match to *ch that sounds like /ch/ as in chain*. This can be played as teams or individuals, depending on how many students are involved. Besides utilizing their short-term memories, students are reading and rereading words they know and verifying their knowledge of the *ch* sound pattern.

Application Routine Showcase: Unscramble It with *wh* Words

Have students reassemble target words that focus on the /wh/ sound of *wh*. Create cards with *wh* words written on them: *whisk, wheat, when, which, whip, whiz, why, whiff*. Create eight cards with *wh* and cards with the following remaining word parts: *i, sk, ea, t, en, i, ch, i, p, i, z, y, i, ff*. Give the students these directions:

Let's repair some words! All the words start with wh. Use the other letter cards to put these words back together:

- *whisk*
- *wheat*
- *when*
- *which*
- *whip*
- *whiz*
- *why*
- *whiff*

CHAPTER SUMMARY

We looked first at consonant sounds, because these letters make fewer different sounds than the vowels. Because so many of the consonants have highly dependable sounds, instruction and practice with these sounds can transfer when students are decoding. We examined:

- Twenty-one letters in the English alphabet that are consonants
- Twenty-five distinct sounds these consonants make
- Eighteen consonant sounds made by single letters
- Seven consonant sounds made by digraphs
- Twenty-one two-letter and three three-letter consonant blends
- Twelve silent consonant pairs

Throughout this chapter we observed the predictability and reliability of the many consonants and consonant patterns. By helping our students see the strength in knowing these patterns we help them become independent readers and autonomous writers. In the next chapter we examine the vowel letters that make nineteen sounds.

Further Reading

David Crystal's book is an interesting read about the history of the English alphabet development (such as *w* was at one time "double *u*").
   Crystal, David. 2012. *Spell It Out: The Curious, Enthralling, and Extraordinary Story of English Spelling*. New York: St. Martin's Press.

The critical role of phonemic awareness as a predictor of individual differences in reading development is examined through a meta-analysis of 235 studies.
   Melby-Lervåg, Monica, Solveig-Alma Halaas Lyster, and Charles Hulme. 2012. "Phonological Skills and Their Role in Learning to Read: A Meta – Analytic Review." *Psychological Bulletin, 138*(2): 322–352.

For research on the order alphabet letter naming and their associated sounds that most commonly occur for young children, the following article suggests typical development as well as instructional guidelines.
   Piasta, Shayne B. 2014. "Moving to Assessment-Guided Differentiated Instruction to Support Young Children's Alphabet Knowledge." *The Reading Teacher, 68*(3): 202–211.

Chapter 4

Vowels: Short, Long, *R*-Controlled, Diphthongs, Schwa, Digraphs

Consonants, you knew pretty much where you stood, but you could never trust a vowel.
– *Maniac Magee* by Jerry Spinelli (1990)

In this chapter we explore facts about vowel sounds – short, long, r-controlled, diphthongs, schwa, and digraphs. As mentioned in the consonant chapter, vowel sounds are unblocked. This means we can draw them out as we say them (try this /eeeeee/ and compare it to /t/). Literacy specialist Denise Eide gives us an easy way to detect the differences between consonants and vowels: "if a sound can easily be sung or shouted **and** your mouth is open, it is a vowel" (2012, 37).

Let's begin with baseline information about the vowel letters and sounds:

- five (and sometimes six) of the twenty-six letters in the English alphabet are vowels
- there are nineteen distinct vowel sounds
- all vowels are voiced (place your fingers on your throat as you say *apple, egg, ice, off, up* to feel the vibration)
- the vowel are sounds represented by multiple combinations (think about the distinct sound of long *a* – you hear it with the letter/combinations a [acorn], a_e [bake], ai [mail], ay [day], ey [they], eigh [sleigh], ei [vein], ea [steak])

- the difference in vowel sounds is created by where we position our tongue (front, mid, back) and the height of the tongue (high to low)
- three different vowel sounds are created when followed by *r*. The vowel sounds are neither long nor short. The sound /är/ has one spelling (*ar – car*), /ôr/ has two spellings (*or – for; our – four*), and /ûr/ has three spellings (*er – her, ir – fir, ur – fur*)
- two of the vowel sounds are diphthongs (*oi/oy* [*boil, toy*] and *ou/ow* [*out, cow*]) that glide
- the schwa (/uh/) is the vowel in the unstressed syllable, can be represented by any of the vowels, and is the most common vowel sound
- as with consonants we have vowel digraphs (two letters to represent one sound – *oo* – /o͞o/ as in *moon*)

Just for Fun

Show students an easy way to distinguish between a long and short vowel sound. How many movements does your mouth make when you slow the sound down? Say /ō/ [as in *toe*] – do you notice your mouth makes two motions? Say **/ŏ/** [as in *hot*] – do you notice your mouth makes only one motion? Try it with all the vowels!

This chapter is organized around the sounds vowels can make, rather than examining the individual letters as we did with consonants. First, unlike the dependable consonants, a vowel letter can make different sounds. Second, examining short vowel sounds first will most likely align with any phonics instruction you are using. Admittedly, vowels can present various problems when decoding and encoding. And we know there are regional accents that can alter any of the following (for instance, I'm thinking of my friend from Virginia's pronunciation of **aunt** [/ah-n-t/] and my Midwest "version" [/ă-n-t/]). But knowing the generalities will assist in choosing the correct vowel letter(s) to represent the vowel sound(s) we hear.

The following sections present the nineteen distinct vowel sounds. The specific vowel sound is in bold (such as /ă/), followed by information pertaining to the pattern, along with other common spellings. These vowel patterns are summarized, with additional examples, in Appendix C for handy reference.

SHORT VOWEL SOUNDS

Most instructional programs begin with short vowel instruction. Short vowel sounds are very common in the English words young learners encounter in their reading. Early texts usually feature consonant-vowel-consonant words such as *cat, bed, sit, dog, mug*. You've likely

Vowels

noticed that English words do not end in a short vowel. This is helpful to remind students when they are decoding: *Do you see a word or syllable that ends in a consonant? Then try the short vowel sound.*

One useful strategy for examining short vowel sounds and expanding the number of words students can orthographically map, is rime family work. While working with first graders, Richard Wylie and Donald Durrell (1970) questioned the value of some of the phonic rules being taught about vowels. This led to questions regarding how hard or easy it is for young readers to learn vowel sounds. Was it easier to learn single vowels (*a*) or whole phonograms (*ack*)? They found stability in learning whole phonograms and that thirty-seven rimes could be the foundation for over 500 words found in primary texts. Of these thirty-seven rimes, twenty-two begin with short vowels (*ack, an, ank, ap, ash, at, ell, est, ick, ill, in, ing, ink, ip, it, ock, op, ot, uck, ug, ump, unk*). We'll explore these rimes further in Chapter 5.

Based on Wylie and Durrell's research, along with the work of other educators, teaching short vowels first is recommended. One reason is, unlike long vowels, most short vowels are represented by single letters. Also, more than half of English words contain short vowels, so they appear more often. The common short vowel sound spellings (with some "anchor words" students can use to compare and contrast what they hear) are:

1. /ă/ as in *apple*
   - when in a CVC (consonant-vowel-consonant) word it is considered dependable in the short *a* sound (*cat, map, de-mand*)
   - short *a* is commonly the first vowel sound taught because of its consistency

2. /ĕ/ as in *elf*
   - when in a CVC (consonant-vowel-consonant) word it is considered dependable in the short *e* sound (*bed*)
   - an additional spelling for the short *e* vowel sound is *ea* (*head, sweat*). This is the only vowel team (*ea*) with a short vowel sound
   - Why do we have *ea* representing /ĕ/? At one time *bread* and *bead* rhymed, as did *head* and *heat*. However, that changed over a 200-year period between Middle and Modern English. Danish linguist Otto Jespersen (1860–1943) first discovered this change and coined it the "Great Vowel Shift." In Arika Okrent's book about oddities in the English language, she shares that over that 200-year period, "the printing press was standardizing and entrenching our spelling habits, [while] the vowel system was undergoing massive reorganization" (2021, 139). In other words, our vowel pronunciations were shifting, but thanks to the printing press our spellings did not change.

> **Anticipated Misunderstanding**
>
> Writers may follow their ear for the /ĕ/ sound of the *ea* spelling. They may represent this short vowel sound with the single letter *e* (*hed, swet*). This is when we return to the strategy discussed in Chapter 3 – use your B.E.E. Now that my "Brain" has predicted to my "Ear" how the word is spelled – does my "Eye" agree? In the case of *hed* and *swet*, do those look right? Practice and time will help students begin to orthographically map this spelling for the short e sound. However, these "near misses" in conventional spelling reassure us that students are listening for the sounds and using their current phonics knowledge to attempt their spellings.

3. /ĭ/ as in *ink*
   - when in a CVC (consonant-vowel-consonant) word it is considered dependable in the short *i* sound (*tin, him*)
   - an additional spelling for the short *i* vowel sound is *y* (*myth*) – these words are Greek in origin (*crypt, hymn, lyric, syrup*)
   - short *i* vowel sound can be confused with short *e* sound (*pin, pen*) so these two short vowel sounds are usually not taught at the same time
   - English words do not end in *i* (see long *i* vowel sound for an explanation)

4. /ŏ/ as in *odd*
   - when in a CVC (consonant-vowel-consonant) word is considered dependable in the short *o* sound (*dog, job, shop*)
   - an additional spelling for short *o* vowel sound is *wa* (*wad, watch*)
   - an additional spelling for short *o* vowel sound is *qua* (*squash, quality*)

5. /ŭ/ as in *up*
   - when in a CVC (consonant-vowel-consonant) word it is considered dependable in the short *u* sound (*cup, sun, must*)
   - an additional spelling for the short *u* sound is *o* (*love, month*)
   - an additional spelling for the short *u* sound is *ou* (*couple, tough*)
   - English words do not end in *u* (see long *u* vowel sound for an explanation)

LONG VOWEL SOUNDS

We often think the long vowel sounds are the easiest to learn, as the vowel letters, unlike consonants, "say their name" – that is the letter name and long vowel sound are the same. So why not teach them first? Long vowel sounds, though easy to hear, can quickly become confusing because there are more letter combinations that represent long vowels than ones that represent short vowels. Remember the long *a* example from above. There are eight letter combinations for long *a*: *a (acorn), a_e (bake), ai (mail), ay (day), ey (they), eigh (sleigh), ei (vein), ea (steak)*. Because of this, and the fact that young readers are more likely to encounter CVC words, where the vowel is usually short, we teach long vowels later when they have developed a bit more readiness for those sounds and the many ways they are represented.

This is a good place to consider the "generalizations," or phonics "rules," we hear such as "when two vowels go walking the first one does the talking." Author confession here . . . when I taught third grade I made a beautiful bulletin board of vowel pairs with arms and legs, walking and holding hands. The first vowel was talking its long sound in a speech bubble. That seemed useful until one of my students asked about *break*. This is where the Science of Reading helps us update our instruction. It also put me on a path to learn more about the English language!

Like me, inspired by a student in his elementary class who continually found exceptions to the rules being taught during reading instruction, Theodore Clymer questioned just how useful such generalizations were. So, Clymer (1963, republished in 1996) examined the rules being taught in "four widely used" (183) reading programs. He found 121 different statements about consonant and vowel generalizations in the four teachers' manuals. He examined all the generalizations and selected forty-five of the most common rules to determine how well they guide the decoding of words. He then chose words from the four reading series and the Gates Reading Vocabulary for the Primary Grades for a total list of 2,600 words. Published in 1935, the Gates Reading Vocabulary for the Primary Grades was created as a guide of suitable words for primary texts. Many basal series used the Gates list as the standard for creating stories and lessons. Clymer wanted to examine how well the rules being taught aligned with words young learners would encounter in their reading. He gave each generalization a "utility" percentage – that is, *how useful is the rule, or how often do words follow that rule*? He calculated the percent of words with that pattern that followed the rule, such as "when two vowels go walking" (in this case, he found it worked only 45% of the time). He established 75% as the level he claimed would make the rule useful for teaching. Through his analyses, Clymer determined that ten generalizations involved consonants (such as, "when *c* and *h* are next to each other, they make only one sound" – this is true 100% of the time). All but one of the ten consonant generalizations were true at least 95% of the time. The generalization of *g* followed by *i* or *e* has the sound of /j/ is true 64% of the time. He found 28 words, such as *give*, as examples of nonconformity. Fortunately, many of the "nonconformers" are words readers can easily remember (*get, girl, begin*).

However, the twenty-four vowel generalizations were much less regular (such as, "the two letters *ow* make the long *o* sound" – which is true 59% of the time, with *down* as an example of a word that did not follow the rule). Of the twenty-four vowel generalizations he found only six occurred at his 75% target rate. The remaining eleven of the forty-five generalizations referred to syllables, with eight above 75% (such as, "in most two-syllable words, the first syllable is accented," which is true 85% of the time). Clymer's intent was to suggest the high-use generalizations that would be worth teaching and avoid the low consistency rules. At the end of his research, he found eighteen useful generalizations. The article about Clymer's study is noted at the end of this chapter under "Further Reading."

Because these generalizations have continued to be referenced since 1963, other researchers sought to replicate his work. Francine Johnston (2001), a researcher with a deep interest in reading and spelling instruction, believed that some of Clymer's rules were poorly stated. One generalization she examined was the "two vowels go walking" rule. She found certain vowel pairs showed more conformity when the pairs were analyzed separately. For example, *ai*, representing long *a*, follows the rule 75% of the time, unlike Clymer's finding that this was true only 45% of the time since his research "lumped" all the vowel teams together. Johnston found the long *a* vowel pair *ay* was the most reliable pattern, being true 96.4% of the time (*day, play, betray, essay*).

One of the common patterns for long vowels is Vowel-Consonant-*e* (VC*e*), where *e* marks the vowel long. Clymer (1963) found this was true only 63% of the time, but Johnston (2001) found differing percentages by once again separating out the patterns. She found for each VC*e* pattern the following percentages followed the VC*e* rule:

- a_e 78% (*face, game, name, grade*)
- e_e 16% (*these, scene, cede, gene*)
- i_e 74% (*bike, dime, kite, mice*)
- o_e 58% (*bone, home, those, note*)
- u_e 77% (*use, cube, huge, June*)

Johnston (2001) concluded, by analyzing each VC*e* combination separately, "teachers can teach the final-*e* generalization with confidence," though she cautioned that "encouraging a flexible strategy will be important" (138).

The flexibility Johnston warns us about becomes essential as we help students understand why there are exceptions to many of these generalities. For instance, recall that English words do not end in *u* (*blue, true, glue*) or *v* (*live, glove, have*) so it is necessary to add the *e*. Another less commonly known rule is *e* has an additional job at the end of words, which is to clarify the word from being mistaken as a plural (*moos/moose, teas/tease, pleas/please, laps/lapse, tens/tense, dens/dense, gees/geese*).

Vowels

Each of the vowel "generalizations" and their percent of consistency Clymer and Johnston found useful are provided in the following list, where appropriate. In Chapter 6 we will discuss syllables, but a rule that is 100% true is every vowel letter has the long sound at the end of an open syllable:

- *pā-per, lā-dy, vol-cā-no*
- *cē-dar, ē-ven, zē-bra, lē-gal*
- *ī-tem, tī-ny, gī-ant, lī-on*
- *ō-pen, ō-mit, car-gō, ō-boe*
- *ū-ni-form, fū-ture, cū-bic, hū-mid*

The common long vowel sound spellings (with some "anchor words" students can use to compare and contrast what they hear) are:

1. /ā/ as in *acorn*
   - Common spellings for long sound of *a* are:
     - *a_e (cake).* Johnston found this true 78% of the time
       - exceptions to the *a_e* pattern are *have* (remember the discussion about no English words ending in *v*) and *are* (which has a historic trail that begins with the Proto-Germanic word "ar")
     - *ai (rain)* and *ay (day).* Johnston found *ay* to be 96.4% reliable and *ai* 75%
   - Other words where we hear long *a* include three less common spellings (*ee* as in *matinee*, *ea* as in *steak*, *eigh* as in *eight*). While long *a* has the highest number of spellings for a long vowel sound, focusing on the three more common patterns (*a_e, ai, ay*) will provide efficient support for young readers as they decode

2. /ē/ as in *equal*
   - Five common spellings for long sound of *e* are:
     - *e* at the end of some single syllable words (*me, be, we*)
     - *ee* as in *feet.* Johnston found this spelling conforms 95.9% of the time. An exception, such as *deer*, is due to the influence of *r* that follows *ee* (see *r*-controlled vowels later)
     - *e_e* as in *these.* There are fewer of these spellings – Johnston found this pattern only 16.6% of the time. Many of the words with this spelling pattern will be vocabulary in more difficult texts – *concrete, scheme, delete, theme*

- *ea* as in *eat*. This spelling is useful 51% of the time (the remaining percentage was discussed above, in the short *e* information about words such as *bread*)
- *y* as in *baby*. Johnston explains "when *y* is used as a vowel in words, it sometimes has the long-*e* sound" in two syllable words. This is true 87% of the time, therefore "a very useful rule" (139)
- A less common spelling of long *e* is *ei* (as in *receive*)

3. /ī/ **as in** *ivy*
   - Four common spellings for long sound of *i* are:
     - *y* as in *fly*. Johnston found this long sound of *y*, at the end of one-syllable words, is 95% reliable (*my, fly, try*). Words derived from these one-syllable words, such as *myself*, also follow the rule
     - *i_e* as in *ride*. Johnston found this occurs 74% of the time
     - *igh* as in *light* and *thigh*. Clymer found this pattern was 100% consistent when the *gh* is silent, making this pattern a highly useful one to teach
     - *ie* as in *pie*. In this case the *e* marks the vowel long and maintains the rule that no English words end in *i*
   - English words do not end in *i*. They may end in the sound (*fly*), but not in the letter. Foreign words are an exception (*macaroni* – Italian, *kiwi* – Māori/New Zealand, *Mississippi* – Ojibwe and Algonquian)

4. /ō/ **as in** *ozone*
   - Two common spellings for long sound of *o* are:
     - *o_e* as in *bone*. Johnston found 58% consistency
     - *ow* as in *snow*. Clymer and Johnston both found this long *o* sound was true only 50% of the time. The other sound for this spelling, as in *cow*, is discussed in Diphthongs

5. /ū/ **as in** *unit*
   - Three common spellings for long sound of *u* are:
     - *u_e* as in *cube*. Johnston found this occurs 77% of the time
     - *ue* as in *true* and *subdue*. This spelling is usually found after a consonant and at the end of a syllable
     - *ew* as in *few*. Clymer found this sound in about 35% of *ew* words and usually occurs in single-syllable words

Vowels

- Very few words end in *u (you)*. Generally, an *e* is added (*blue*). Words may have been borrowed from other languages (Southern Bushman – *gnu*, Portuguese – *emu*, French – *menu*) or are a shortened form (*flu – influenza*)

Just For Fun

When an author systematically omits a certain letter of the alphabet, it is called a lipogram. Ernest Vincent Wright (1939) wrote *Gadsby: A Story of Over 50,000 Words Without Using the Letter "E."* In the book's opening Wright describes how, even though *e* is the most commonly used letter, he tied down the *e* key on his typewriter to be sure he never used it. Show students two or three sentences from a text you are using (Science, free reading, Social Studies) and work together to rewrite them so the letter *e* is not used. How easy was it?

R-CONTROLLED VOWEL SOUNDS

Many programs call this sound "Bossy R" to point out the influence the letter *r* has over the vowel sound. This is taught after students are familiar with the short and long vowel sounds so they can differentiate the *r*-controlled ones. This is also one of the sound generalizations that can be influenced greatly by regional dialects. The following information presents a Midwest accent that tends to have a bit less dialectical differences, but be aware of what works for your population of students.

While there are five common spellings for *r*-controlled vowels (*ar, er, ir, or, ur*), there are three distinct sounds – /är/, /ôr/, and /ûr/. In all cases, the vowel and the *r* create one sound (that is, they are not separated when saying them aloud). The three sounds and their spellings are:

1. **/är/ as in *car***
   - this is generally the first *r*-controlled vowel taught due to its own, distinct sound 89% of the time (*arm, star, spark, March*)
   - some phonics programs will point out other spellings, which slightly shifts how this *r*-controlled vowel sounds and may or may not work regionally:
     - – *air* as in *chair, stair, hair*
     - – *are* as in *care, dare, square*

Anticipated Misunderstanding

When students spell words with *-ar* they may omit the *-a* (*frm/farm, hrd/hard*). They are "hearing" the letter name, *r*, even though, unlike vowels, consonant sounds are not the name of the letter. Here we can remind students every syllable must have vowel letter(s) to represent the vowel sound . . . what is missing? Slow it down – what *vowel sound* does the *r* make? Is that what your spelling shows?

2. **/ôr/ as in corn**
    - this is the next frequently distinct sound which occurs 41% of the time (*for, north, torch*)
    - students should be familiar with the high frequency word *or*, so they can use that to help them "hear" the *r*-controlled vowel in words such as *orbit, force, story*
    - – *or* may appear at the end of nouns (*actor, doctor, mayor, tutor, senator*)
    - – *or* is generally attached to Latin verbs that end in *-ate* (*elevate/elevator, incubate/incubator*)
    - some phonics programs point out other spellings and may or may not work regionally:
        - – *ore* as in *chore, bore, fore*
        - – *oor* as in *floor, door, boor*
        - – *oar* as in *soar, roar, boar*

> **Just for Fun**
>
> British words include *-our*, as in *behaviour* and *colour*, whereas American English spellings do not (*behavior, color*). We have Daniel Webster to thank for that. Webster changed the spellings of some words to purposefully differ our American version from British English. In 1798 he called for a language for our country, now independent from Great Britain. Webster said, "*Now* is the time, and *this* the country . . . Let us then seize the present moment, and establish a *national language*, as well as a national government" (Martin 2019, unpaged). Among Webster's other changes were *re* words to *er* (*theatre/theater*), *s* to *z* (*organise/organize*), *ce* to *se* (*defence/defense*), and dropping *k* (*musick/music*).

3. **/ûr/ as in *her, hurt, dirt***
    - – *er* spelling of the */ûr/* sound occurs 40% of the time (*her, enter, term*)
        - – *er* is added to Old English words to create a noun meaning "person who has to do with" (*teacher, worker, singer, lawyer, baker*)
        - – *er* is added to the end of words for comparison (*taller, cleaner, funnier*)
    - – *ur* spelling of the */ûr/* sound occurs 26% of the time (*curl, surf, curve*)
        - an additional spelling includes *-ure* and connects back to Old French, meaning "make use of, bring about" (*pleasure, mixture, rapture*)
        - – *ur* appears in two days of the week (*Thursday, Saturday*)
    - – *ir* spelling of the */ûr/* sound occurs 13% of the time (*sir, girl, shirt*)
        - is the least common spelling, but often seen in early texts (*bird, dirt, third, girl*)

Vowels

- many words spelled this way are related to ones where we hear /ī/ (*admiration/admire, expiration/expire, inspiration/inspire*)
- words from the root "circ" use -*ir* (*circle, circular, circus, circuit*)

> **Anticipated Misunderstanding**
>
> It is not unusual for students to flip the *r* and the vowel it influences when they write. We might see them spell *gril* for *girl*, *crul* for *curl*, and *frot* for *fort*. We discussed consonant liquids (*r*, *l*) in Chapter 3 – those letters that seem to float in the mouth. This can influence how they are hearing these *r*-controlled vowels and often will anticipate the spelling is the consonant blend (*gr*, *br*) instead of the *r*-controlled vowel. Because these *r*-controlled vowels are often difficult to hear, time and practice will change their spelling attempts.

DIPHTHONGS

A diphthong is a single vowel sound that is written with two letters. There are two vowel diphthongs. As we blend the vowels we create a gliding sound.

1. /ow/ as in *cow* and *sound*
   - the *ow* spelling for the /ow/ diphthong occurs 56% of the time and tends to be at the end of words
   - the *ow* spelling is also associated with /ō/, so we often ask students to try both when decoding to listen to which one seems correct for the text they are reading
   - the *ou* spelling for the /ow/ diphthong occurs 29% of the time and tends to be inside the word or syllable, unless the word rhymes with *down* or *owl* (*frown, howl, towel*) and then the *ow* spelling is used

2. /oi/ as in *boil* and *toy*
   - Johnston found the *oi* spelling is true 100% of the time for this sound
     - *oi* is not found at the end of English words (Hawaiian food – *poi*, Japanese fish – *koi*)
   - Johnston found the *oy* spelling is true 100% of the time for this sound and may be in the middle (*loyal*) or at the end (*toy*) of a word

SCHWA

Say these words aloud, listening to the vowel in bold . . . **a**go, it**e**m, fam**i**ly, **o**ven, **u**pon. What do you notice? Each vowel says /uh/! Easy to say . . . a little harder to predict when writing words because any of the vowel letters can represent the schwa sound.

1. /ə/
    - The schwa is the vowel sound, in the unstressed syllable
    - It is the most common vowel sound in English (more than 80% of two-syllable words contain a schwa sound)
    - all five vowels sound identical in this position
    - while prevalent in multi-syllable words, some single-syllable words contain schwa, which makes sentence reading fluent, as we can quickly read the words (*a, the, of, was*)

DIGRAPHS

As with consonant digraphs, vowel digraphs create a new sound. While we have looked at some two-letter combinations to create various vowel sounds (/ā/ spelled *ai*, /ō/ spelled *oa*), in this last section we look at three combinations that have special sounds in English words.

1. /aw/ as in *crawl* and *author*
    - often described as complex vowel combinations
    - *au* appears at the beginning or middle of words (*autumn, auction, fault, sauce*), but never at the end
    - *aw* can be found at the beginning, middle, or end of words (*awesome, lawn, draw*)
    - *aw* and *au* may seem to have the short *o* vowel sound (*claw, launch*) in some regional variants

2. /o͞o/ as in *mood*
    - classified as the long sound of *oo*, is the most common, occurring 56% of the time
    - sounds similar to long *u*

3. /o͝o/ as in *book*
    - considered the short sound of *oo*, occurring 36% of the time
    - sounds similar to short *u*
    - always before *k*, as in l**oo**k, c**oo**k, sh**oo**k, br**oo**k

You will notice the *oo* percentage accounts for 92% of English words with that spelling. The remaining percent includes words like *floor* and *blood*. Like other words we wonder about, the history of English provides the answer. For instance, *blood* comes from Old Saxon *blôd*, preserving how it was said all those years ago. *Floor* has its history in Old Norse *flor*. But generally,

Vowels

we have two sounds of *oo*. But which to pick when reading? Nearly forty years ago Margaret Bishop, a language specialist, compiled a reference book for phonics and spelling. Bishop examined several word lists, such as those from Hanna, Hanna, and Hodges, who we discussed in Chapter 3. From those lists she chose words she believed were most likely seen in school texts. She did a number count of words for each phonic sound, listing regular or irregular ones. Her recommendation concerning /ōō/ and /ŏŏ/ was: "There is no way to predict whether an OO will be long or short. However, novices need only learn the long sound since this will bring them close enough to the correct sound to get the meaning even when the OO turns out to be short" (1986, 184). Since /ōō/ has a higher usage, this is good advice. This is also helpful to think about regarding some of the other vowel sounds and their generalizations described above. Which ones should a student try first when decoding? Which are most reliable? Creating charts and examples students can refer to will facilitate memories about the sounds and help with orthographic mapping.

APPLICATION ROUTINES IN ACTION

Here are three examples of Application Routines students can engage in for more practice with the vowel patterns we have just examined. You will want to choose patterns or words that connect to your vowel instruction. Also, these examples may need a bit of adjusting for your population.

Application Routine Showcase: Sort It with Final *y*

Create a closed sort by making cards or sticky notes with the following words: *play, stay, tray, delay, city, icy, party, only, cry, reply, spy, why*. Write three key words on posters, bulletin board, whiteboard, or 8 ½ × 11 paper (depending on space availability and how large a group will be doing the sort). Label three separate areas with the key words: *January, May, July*. Mix the word cards and give students these directions: *Read each card, listen to the y at the end of the word and place it in the month that has the same y sound. (January – icy, party, only; May – play, stay, tray; July – cry, spy, why)*. Give each student two blank cards or sticky notes and ask them to think of a word they could add to one or two of the months that have the same *y* sound. You can also use this as an open sort by not giving students the key words. After sorting, guide the student to help write the generalization: *when y is a vowel, it has three sounds, long e, long a, and long i. The long a sound is always spelled ay*. The words used in this sort may seem "easy," but there are important reasons for choosing words such as these. First, the students can quickly and easily read them, thus expediting the actual sorting. Second, they can "get inside" a word with which they are familiar. Think of it as being comfortable with old friends – we know the words, we know we can work with them, and we can focus on listening and looking for the target pattern. Word choices in sorts are critical to successfully reaching the intended purpose. Be certain to choose words your students can confidently read.

Application Routine Showcase: Build It with Vowel Patterns

Using letter tiles or slips of paper, give students the letters *r, n, st, s, p, m, w, bl* and vowel patterns *ai, ea, oa, ow, ue.* They will be building *rain, east, soap, mow, blue.* Display the letters and vowel patterns where everyone can see the letters. Show the list of target words and work together to build them. Ask what they notice about the five vowel patterns (all are long vowel sounds). Next, let the students make suggestions of how they can use the letters to make other words, reminding them all words must have the long vowel sound. For instance, they might suggest *waist, stain, pain, steam, heap, roam, roast, blow, row, sow, stow, row, sue.* If the students are having difficulty seeing other words, move a few letters around to help. For instance, show if you take *east* and move the *st* before the *ea* and add *m* you create a new word (*steam*). You can continue to do this in a supportive way to build words – remove the *m* from *mow* and ask if they see any consonants you could use in place of *m* (*r, st, s*). If students suggest *n* or *h*, make the words and then ask them to read them aloud. *Now* and *how* have the diphthong sound, as in *cow*.

Application Routine Showcase: Match It with *R*-Controlled Vowels

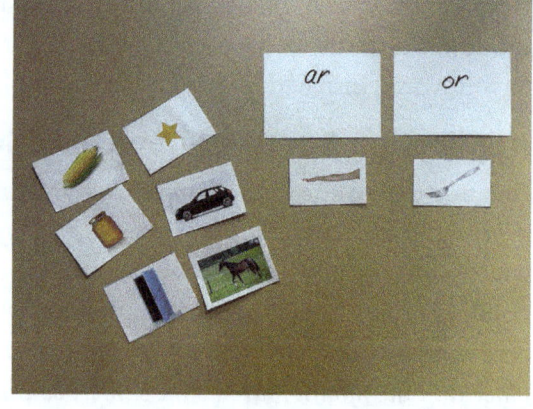

Have students match pictures of *r*-controlled words to the correct spelling. Print pictures of *arm, car, star, heart, jar, corn, fork, horse, door, orange.* Some free resources for pictures or drawings for classroom use are Google images, Pixabay, or Unsplash. Make five cards labeled *ar* and five cards labeled *or.* A fun way to do this matching is to pass out the pictures and *r*-controlled cards to individuals. The students with the ten picture cards and the ones with the *r*-controlled cards need to find each other. Once they have matched, give each pair a sticky note and ask them to write the word of the picture they have (this way, you can pull the sticky note off the picture and reuse this "Match it" for side work). Last, have the two groups (*ar, or*) get together and brainstorm other words that include their *r*-controlled pattern.

CHAPTER SUMMARY

This chapter examined six vowel sound categories: short, long, *r*-controlled, diphthongs, schwa, and digraphs. This information provides specifics about the nineteen vowel sounds using the five vowel letters, plus *y* where applicable. The variable use of vowels in English can present challenges to readers. But, consistencies do exist, and focusing instruction and practice on these generalities will broaden students' ability to decode and encode. Undoubtedly, multiple experiences with these vowel patterns will support learners in orthographically mapping sounds to letters. In the next chapter we will explore the rime families as a way to expand word knowledge.

Further Reading

Theodore Clymer's landmark study of teaching phonic generalizations is described in the 1963 article (republished in 1996). He shares his methods, results, and the forty-five generalizations:
   Clymer, Theodore. 1963/1996. "The Utility of Phonic Generalizations in the Primary Grades." *The Reading Teacher, 16/50*: 252–258/182–185.

An excellent analysis and extension of Clymer's study regarding vowel generalizations is:
   Johnston, Francine. 2001. "The Utility of Phonic Generalizations: Let's Take another Look at Clymer's Conclusions." *The Reading Teacher, 55*(2): 132–143.

For an entertaining and joyful look at the history of English, linguistics Professor Arkia Okrent offers a fast-paced read:
   Okrent, Arika. 2021. *Highly Irregular: Why Tough, Through, and Dough Don't Rhyme and Other Oddities of the English Language*. Illustrated by Sean O'Neill. New York: Oxford University Press.

The thirty-seven rimes (or phonograms, as referred to in their article) are available in the original work of Richard Wylie and Donald Durrell.
   Wylie, Richard, and Donald Durrell. 1970. "Teaching Vowels through Phonograms." *Elementary English, 47*: 787–791.

Chapter 5

Onsets and Rimes

Man does not live by words alone, despite the fact that sometimes he has to eat them.
– Adlai E. Stevenson, Jr. (1900–1965)

Most instructional reading programs give attention to phonograms. Phonograms have a specific letter-sound relationship (*-ay, -est, -ight, -ock, -ug*) and represent one syllable. A phonogram is, according to the Merriam-Webster Dictionary, (2025, unpaged) "a succession of orthographic letters that occurs with the same phonetic value in several words (such as the *ight* of *bright, fight,* and *flight*)" (unpaged). The linguistic term more commonly used today is "rime," although some programs may simply call them "word families."

In the International Literacy Association Glossary, a rime is "the part of a syllable that includes the vowel and all subsequent sounds in the syllable" (2025, unpaged). Consonants are added before the rime and are called the onset (***d**-ay, **cr**-est, **l**-ight, **sh**-ock, **shr**-ug*). Onsets can be single consonants (***d***-ay), consonant blends (***shr***-ug), or digraphs (***sh***-ock). The rimes also appear in more complex multisyllabic words, thus expanding their usefulness in learning to decode (*att-**ack**, det-**ail**, rem-**ain***).

WHY RIME INSTRUCTION IS IMPORTANT

We travel back to 1970 to understand how we learned the value of teaching phonograms. Richard Wylie and Donald Durrell took a close look at how to better help students learn to read. They examined Clymer's 1963 rules (discussed in Chapter 3 – Vowels) and found the "lack of dependability for vowel rules in intermediate grade words" (787) as one of the problems learners encounter. After working with 900 first graders, they discovered focusing on ending phonograms gave vowel stability to word learning. They suggested thirty-seven vowel phonograms were dependable (See Table 5.1). They found 500 primary grade words "are derived from these thirty-seven high-frequency phonograms" (787–788), making them highly useful to teach.

Table 5.1 Wylie and Durrell's 37 Phonograms
Source: Wylie, Richard E. and Donald D. Durrell. 1970. "Teaching Vowels Through Phonograms." *Elementary English*, 47: 787–791.

-ack	-ail	-ain	-ake	-ale	-ame
-an	-ank	-ap	-ash	-at	-ate
-aw	-ay	-eat	-ell	-est	-ice
-ick	-ide	-ight	-ill	-in	-ine
-ing	-ink	-ip	-it	-ock	-oke
-op	-ore	-ot	-uck	-ug	-ump
-unk					

Marilyn Adams, a specialist in cognition and linguistics, further explained the value in considering phonograms. She notes, "the onset and rime are relatively easy to remember and to splice back together. Yet another advantage of exploiting phonograms in decoding instruction is that they provide a means of introducing and exercising many primer words with relative efficiency" (1990, 321).

Usha Goswami, a neuroscientist, "suggests that rhythm is the hidden factor in how children learn and process speech" (Yidan Prize 2024, unpaged). Through Goswami's research (1991), she found that children's "onset-rime segmentation skills – are intimately connected with their ability to learn about letter sequences when they begin reading" (1121). Louisa Cook Moats, the linguistic expert mentioned in Chapter 3, comments that the mind "is always seeking pattern recognition to reduce the load on memory and facilitate retrieval of linguistic information" (2001, 72).

Onsets and Rimes

Both Goswami and Moats help us see the value in looking for and learning the rime family patterns of English. Rimes allow students to more efficiently learn short vowel sounds since the phonograms offer what we call stability. Students become familiar with stable "chunks" of words that facilitate decoding and encoding fluency.

THE THIRTY-SEVEN RIMES

Combining the rimes with your vowel instruction gives students powerful ways to work across words as they read and write. Goswami claims, "phonological skills at the onset-rime level may help children to become aware of the functional importance of rime units in the orthography" (2000, 263). That is to say, students' awareness of rimes not only improves reading fluency, but aids in their understanding of spelling conventions.

As we consider using the rimes in our phonics instruction, we can group the reliable vowel sounds found in Wylie and Durrell's (1970) thirty-seven phonograms as:

- twenty-two short vowels
  - *ack, -an, -ank, -ap, -ash, -at, -ell, -est, -ick, -ill, -in, -ing, -ink, -ip, -it, -ock, -op, -ot, -uck, -ug, -ump, -unk*
- thirteen long vowels
  - *ail, -ain, -ake, -ale, -ame, -ate, -ay, -eat, -ice, -ide, -ight, -ine, -oke*
- one digraph
  - *aw*
- one r-controlled
  - *ore*

The rimes identified by Wylie and Durrell are grouped in the following chart, along with suggested words. The words are presented in two groups. The first column is single consonants plus the rime, the second is consonant blends and digraphs plus the rime. In this way, you can differentiate as needed for your students. The words are suggestions to get you started and provide support for the Application Routines. You may choose to add more complex words to these lists from your students' content reading (for example, Science: *jackal, snowflake, icecap, habitat*; Social Studies: *Shaker, Canyon, capitol, Democrat, latitude*; Language Arts: *email, explain, format, folktale*). Invite students to contribute words they come across in their personal reading (be**fore**, be**came**, ha**ppy**, de**bate**, holi**day**).

Six Short *a* Rimes

-ack		-an		-ank		-ap		-ash		-at	
back	black	an	bran	bank	blank	cap	chap	bash	brash	bat	brat
hack	clack	ban	clan	dank	clank	gap	clap	cash	clash	cat	chat
jack	crack	can	flan	Hank	crank	lap	flap	dash	crash	fat	drat
lack	flack	Dan	Fran	rank	drank	map	scrap	gash	flash	hat	flat
pack	knack	fan	plan	sank	flank	nap	slap	hash	gnash	mat	gnat
quack	shack	Jan	scan	tank	frank	rap	snap	lash	slash	pat	scat
rack	smack	man	slant	yank	plank	sap	strap	mash	smash	rat	slat
sack	snack	Nan	span		prank	tap	trap	rash	splash	sat	splat
tack	stack	pan	Stan		shank	yap	wrap	sash	stash	vat	sprat
	track	ran	than		spank	zap			thrash		that
	whack	tan			stank				trash		
		van			swank						
					thank						

Just for Fun

Students might wonder about the word *yak* – as it sounds like the *-ack* phonogram but is not spelled that way. "We know 'ck' follows a short-vowel sound (such as *back*; words with a long-vowel end in 'k' – such as *peek*). So what about *yak*? We turn to the word's origin. *Yak* is an English version of a Tibetan word – *g-yag* – which means 'wild ox of Central Asia.' English adopted the word" (Harrison, Rasinski, and Fresch 2022a, 19).

Two Short *e* Rimes

-ell		-est	
bell	dwell	best	blest
cell	knell	fest	chest
dell	shell	jest	crest
fell	smell	nest	wrest
jell	spell	pest	
Nell	swell	quest	
quell		rest	
sell		test	
tell		vest	
well		west	
yell		zest	

Onsets and Rimes

Seven Short *i* Rimes

-ick		-ill		-in		-ing		-ink		-ip		-it	
kick	brick	bill	chill	bin	grin	Bing	bling	kink	blink	dip	blip	bit	flit
lick	chick	dill	drill	din	chin	ding	bring	link	brink	hip	chip	fit	grit
Mick	click	fill	frill	fin	shin	king	cling	mink	chink	lip	clip	hit	knit
Nick	crick	gill	grill	in	skin	ping	fling	pink	clink	nip	drip	kit	skit
pick	flick	hill	krill	kin	spin	ring	sling	rink	drink	pip	flip	lit	slit
quick	slick	ill	shrill	pin	thin	sing	spring	sink	plink	quip	grip	nit	spit
Rick	stick	Jill	skill	sin	twin	ting	sting	wink	shrink	rip	ship	pit	split
sick	thick	kill	spill	tin		wing	string		skink	sip	skip	quit	
tick	trick	mill	still	win		zing	swing		slink	tip	slip	sit	
wick		pill	swill				thing		stink	yip	snip	wit	
		quill	thrill				wring		think	zip	strip	zit	
		rill	trill								trip		
		sill	twill								whip		
		till											
		will											

Three Short *o* Rimes

-ock		-op		-ot	
dock	block	bop	chop	cot	blot
hock	chock	cop	crop	dot	clot
jock	clock	hop	drop	got	knot
lock	crock	lop	flop	hot	plot
mock	flock	mop	glop	jot	shot
rock	frock	pop	plop	lot	slot
sock	knock	sop	prop	not	snot
tock	shock	top	shop	pot	spot
	smock		slop	rot	trot
	stock		stop	sot	
				tot	

Four Short *u* Rimes

-uck		-ug		-ump		-unk	
buck	chuck	bug	chug	bump	chump	bunk	chunk
duck	cluck	dug	drug	dump	clump	dunk	clunk
luck	pluck	hug	glug	hump	frump	funk	drunk
muck	shuck	jug	plug	jump	grump	gunk	flunk
puck	snuck	lug	shrug	lump	plump	hunk	plunk
suck	stuck	mug	slug	pump	slump	junk	shrunk
tuck	struck	pug	smug	rump	stump	punk	skunk
yuck	truck	rug	snug	sump	thump	sunk	slunk
		tug	thug	ump	trump		spunk
					whump		stunk
							trunk

Seven Long *a* Rimes

-ail		-ain		-ake		-ale		-ame		-ate		-ay	
fail	frail	gain	brain	bake	Blake	bale	scale	came	blame	date	crate	bay	bray
Gail	grail	lain	chain	cake	brake	dale	shale	dame	flame	fate	grate	day	clay
hail	snail	main	drain	fake	drake	gale	stale	fame	frame	gate	plate	gay	fray
jail	trail	pain	faint	Jake	flake	hale	whale	game	shame	hate	skate	hay	gray
mail		rain	grain	lake	shake	kale		lame		Kate	slate	Jay	play
nail		vain	plain	make	snake	male		name		late	state	lay	pray
pail			paint	quake	stake	pale		same		mate		may	slay
quail			slain	rake		sale		tame		Nate		nay	spray
rail			Spain	sake		tale				rate		pay	stay
sail			sprain	take		vale						ray	stray
tail			stain	wake		yale						say	sway
wail			strain									way	tray
			train										

Onsets and Rimes

One Long *e* Rime

-eat	
beat	bleat
eat	cheat
feat	cleat
heat	pleat
meat	treat
neat	wheat
peat	
seat	

Just for Fun

Wonder why *great* doesn't have the same vowel sound as *beat*? Remember the discussion in Chapter 4 about Otto Jespersen's discovery of the "Great Vowel Shift"? Over a 200-year period from Middle to Modern English some vowel sounds "shifted" in where we pronounced them in our mouths. *Great* is an example of a word that changed in pronunciation, but because of the printing press the spelling did not change. This is the only "vowel team" (*-ea*) that can represent a short vowel. Ask students to think of other words where *ea* represents the /ĕ/ sound (such as *bread, deaf, dealt, head, heavy*). Many of these words "are related to words in which EA is long (*heave-heavy, deal-dealt, mean-meant, please-pleasure*)" (Bishop 1986, 115).

Four Long *i* Rimes

-ice		*-ide*		*-ight*		*-ine*	
dice	price	bide	bride	fight	blight	dine	brine
lice	slice	hide	chide	light	bright	fine	shine
mice	spice	ride	glide	might	flight	line	shrine
nice	splice	side	pride	night	fright	mine	spine
rice	thrice	tide	slide	right	knight	nine	swine
vice	twice	wide	snide	sight	plight	pine	thine
			stride	tight	slight	tine	twine
						vine	whine
						wine	

One Long *o* Rime

-oke	
coke	bloke
joke	broke
poke	choke
woke	smoke
yoke	spoke
	stoke
	stroke

One Vowel Digraph Rime

-aw	
caw	claw
jaw	craw
law	draw
paw	flaw
raw	gnaw
saw	slaw
	squaw
	straw
	thaw

One *r*-Controlled Rime

-ore	
bore	chore
core	score
fore	shore
gore	snore
lore	spore
more	store
pore	swore
sore	
tore	
wore	
yore	

Onsets and Rimes

RESOURCES FOR MORE WORDS

Looking for more words? Here are a few suggestions.

For a variety of word lists for instructional purposes:

- Jacqueline E. Kress and Edward Fry. 2015 – *The Reading Teacher's Book of Lists, 6th Edition.*

For grade-leveled word lists organized by phonics features:

- Mary Jo Fresch and Aileen Wheaton. 2019 – *The Spelling List and Word Study Resource Book: Organized Spelling Lists, Greek and Latin Roots, Word Histories, and other Resources for Dynamic Spelling and Vocabulary Instruction.*

For a large corpus of words classified by "frequency and percentage tabulation of phoneme-grapheme correspondences" (15):

- Hanna, Hanna, Hodges, and Rudorf report (discussed in Chapter 3). 1966 – *Phoneme-grapheme Correspondences as Cues to Spelling Improvement.* Available at eric.ed.gov.

Texas SPED also provides lists of words with specific phonograms at the link in the QR code.

APPLICATION ROUTINES IN ACTION

The thirty-seven rimes are highly useful because they appear in so many words students will read and write. Finding ways to apply what they are learning is critical for developing automaticity in word recognition. Here are three Application Routine examples that will get you started following your instruction.

Application Routine Showcase: Build It with Five Rimes

This is ideal for small groups. Using letter tiles or slips of paper, give each group two each of the letters *g, l, m, n, fl*. Make five each of the following rime cards: *ame, ice, oat*. Ask students to build as many words as they can, using the letters and rimes. Have a list ready to share with them if they

get stumped (*game, lame, name, flame, lice, mice, nice, goat, moat, float*). They will have extra rime cards left (*ame, ice, ice, oat, oat*). Ask them to write their own onsets to make other words (such as *same, dice, coat*).

Application Routine Showcase: Unscramble It Using Six Rimes

Have students assemble onsets and rimes. Make multiple copies of six onset cards: *b, f, j, l, n, s* and six rime cards: *-ack, -ell, -eed, -ice, -ill, -ug*. Ask students to see how many real words they can make (*back, jack, lack, sack, bell, fell, sell, feed, need, seed, lice, nice, bill, fill, sill, bug, jug, lug*). Ask them to assist in writing a list of words they find. If you're leading this as a whole class activity you can extend it by showing just the rimes and asking students for other words they know beyond the ones they found during the routine.

Application Routine Showcase: Match It with Short and Long *a*

Have students match rime words with their vowel sounds. Create word cards: *game, stay, gate, chain, lamp, bag, tab, jam*. Create four each of the vowel sounds with a key word to help: /ā/ *as in acorn* and /ă/ *as in apple*. Review with students the differences in the two vowel sounds. Distribute the word and vowel sound cards to the class. If you have more students than cards, have two of them buddy up with one card (this is a good way to provide support for a shy student or one who may be unsure of the words and vowel sounds). Ask students to walk around to find a match for the word and vowel sound. Once they have paired up, ask students to read their word and the sound of *a* that it makes. Invite the pairs to think of other words with their rime and make a list for them to view.

CHAPTER SUMMARY

This chapter presented the rationale for focusing on Wylie and Durrell's (1970) thirty-seven phonograms. Offered as highly useful for instruction due to vowel stability, the phonograms (or rimes) are found in over 500 primary words. Learning these "chunks" facilitates decoding and encoding. There is an efficiency that develops as students begin to instantly recognize the rime (or, phonogram), allowing them to blend the consonant onsets. Without doubt, utilizing these rimes/phonograms/word families helps students expand their skills for sounding across words.

Further Reading

Edward Fry also explored phonograms, finding that teaching them is a highly useful way for students to learn. His work yielded thirty-eight common phonograms, which he ranked by frequency in primary words. Wylie, Durrell, and Fry's lists have twenty-six phonograms in common. To find "relatively common example words"

Onsets and Rimes

(621), Fry used two rhyming dictionaries and a dissertation on the topic and found twelve different, additional phonograms.

Fry, Edward. 1998. "The Most Common Phonograms." *The Reading Teacher, 51*(7): 620–622.

Usha Goswami's research points out the value in learning rimes:

Goswami, Usha. 2000. "Phonological and Lexical Processes." In *Handbook of Reading Research Volume III*, edited by Michael L. Kamil, Peter B. Mosenthal, P. David Pearson, and Rebecca Barr, 251–267. New York: Routledge.

Rime family poetry, word ladders, and lessons are the focus of these two books:

- Harrison, David L., Timothy V. Rasinski, and Mary Jo Fresch. 2022a. *Partner Poems & Word Ladders for Building Foundational Literacy Skills, Grades K-2*. New York: Scholastic.

- Harrison, David L., Timothy V. Rasinski, and Mary Jo Fresch. 2022b. *Partner Poems & Word Ladders for Building Foundational Literacy Skills, Grades 1–3*. New York: Scholastic.

Chapter 6

Syllables

To learn to read is to light a fire; every syllable that is spelled out is a spark.

– Victor Hugo (1802–1885)

As students become more secure in their phonics knowledge, instruction should include understanding how words are divided into syllables. As students learn to sound across words, we ask them the number of vowel sounds they hear. For every vowel sound we hear there is one syllable (*boat – oa – /ō/ –* one syllable*; ti-ger – /ī/* and */ûr/ –* two syllables). There may be more than one vowel letter (such as the *oa* in *boat*), but there is only one vowel sound (/ō/) in each syllable. Paying attention to how many syllables they hear is an important listening task that influences students' reading and spelling success.

WHY DO SYLLABLES MATTER?

Recognizing syllables serves two purposes. First, knowing how to break a word into syllables is a more efficient way to read unknown words. We can consider affix meanings to help decode (*semi-* means *half, -ful* means *to be full*). Second, saying a word by syllables assists in spelling attempts. By decoding words according to six syllable types, students learn ways to recognize whether a vowel is long or short. Studies have shown that interventions for struggling readers that include instruction in syllables improved reading skills. Jennifer Diliberto, a researcher focused on ways to assist struggling readers, offered direct instruction about syllables to half a class of middle school students. The research group who received the instruction included students with attention deficit hyperactivity disorder (ADHD) and who were at risk for reading failure. Over the six month period Diliberto and her team of researchers found improvement in "word identification, word attack, and reading comprehension" (2008, 14). They concluded that "students with high incidence disabilities, including ADHD, and those students at risk for reading failure benefited from systematic intervention" (2008, 25). The students showed gains in their word attack skills and reading comprehension after learning to break multisyllabic words into decodable chunks. Helping students move beyond letter by letter decoding and encoding adds accuracy and efficiency to their reading and spelling attempts.

In the previous chapter we looked at the value of learning the phonograms (rimes) that give stability to short vowels. These rime "chunks" facilitate reading and writing. We hear the one vowel sound, knowing the word has one syllable. However, where do we begin if we are unfamiliar with a multisyllabic word? Breaking it into syllables is a more efficient way to sound it out. Learning how to break multisyllabic words is critical as students encounter more complex text.

Syllables also help us figure out the meaning of certain words as we pay attention to context and listen to which syllable is stressed when spoken. Words that are spelled the same but differ in pronunciation, meaning, and origin are called heteronyms. Let's examine this word – *heter-* means "other, different" and *-nym* means "name." So, "different names" for the same word. While single syllable heteronyms such as *wind*, as "air in motion" and as "move by turning and twisting" change in pronunciation, differences in heteronyms are even more evident in multisyllabic words where the accent shifts. This is where knowing about syllables helps. If I see *minute* in print, context will need to help me divide the word into two syllables. The word could have an open syllable: /mī/ /nūt/ (small) or a closed syllable: /mĭn/ /ĭt/ (time passing). We "re**cord**" our voices singing and we can set a world "**re**cord" at an Olympic event. We "re**fuse**" to litter so we make sure the "**re**fuse" goes in the trash bin. They will "per**mit**" us to have the street party once we get a "**per**mit." We'll learn more about these types of words in Chapter 7, but knowing the difference in syllable stress is important when comprehending text.

TEACHING SYLLABLES

Generally, examination of syllables begins once students have a working knowledge of consonant and vowel sounds. This makes decoding and encoding manageable. We may begin with simple activities to help students hear parts to more complex ones that require syllabication and designation of which syllable is stressed. Literacy educators Mary and James Rycik remind us that the goal "is to help students become more proficient at reading and writing words, not become an expert in syllable division" (2007, 121). By moving beyond letter by letter decoding and paying close attention to syllables, students add fluency to not only their reading but also their spelling attempts.

Syllables

There are several ways to teach syllables. First, a common approach asks students to clap as they slowly say the word – *blue* (clap), *pumpkin* – *pump* (clap) *kin* (clap), *birthday* – *birth* (clap) *day* (clap). Children often begin with their names as a familiar word to clap. Our modeling of how to do this is key in helping students pay attention to syllables. Some educators believe this may be a problematic way to instruct because it requires simultaneous coordination of hearing the syllables and the physical movement of clapping. As well, young learners may not yet have developed the phonemic awareness to hear the syllables.

A second approach to allow students to listen for syllables in unknown words, is to have children put their hands lightly under their chin. They say the word and feel the number of times their jaw "drops" and bumps their hand. Put your hand under your chin and say *blue*. Now say *pumpkin*. Feel the difference in the number of times your jaw dropped to touch your hand? Many young learners find this has a tactile quality that helps in physically sensing the number of syllables.

A third approach is suggested by Denise Eide, whose English language focus we have considered before. She suggests humming the word. In Chapter 3 – Vowels, Eide suggested if you could sing the sound, it is a vowel. When we hum, we "sing" the vowel. There is only one per syllable, so we count our humming. Try these . . . *tiger* (hum-hum), *alphabet* (hum, hum, hum), *cat* (hum). Practice such as this can also draw attention to affixes (*re-run* [hum hum] – to run again, *illegal* [hum, hum hum] – not legal, *careful* [hum hum] – full of care). Reading fluency and vocabulary development are both served in learning to pay attention to these syllables that are affixes.

Just for Fun

Challenge students with words that have a certain number of syllables. They must match the word to the syllable description given, such as:
- two months that have four syllables (January, February)
- three months that have one syllable (March, May, June)
- the only state name that is one syllable (Maine)
- a sport that is two syllables (baseball, soccer, football, rugby, tennis, bowling, hockey)
- colors that have two syllables (yellow, purple, navy, amber, scarlet, olive)
- animals that have one syllable (dog, cat, bird, bat, owl, ape, shark, seal, yak)

TYPES OF SYLLABLES

There are six different types of syllables. Looking at the differing types is a useful skill for our reading and spelling. Linguist Louisa Cook Moats suggests that knowing syllable types is important "because they encourage students to notice similar chunks of print when they are developing automatic word recognition and spelling skills" (2001, 99).

Before examining the six types, here are some "big picture" rules about syllables:

- each syllable has one vowel sound – /b//ō//t/ – *boat* (1 vowel sound, 1 syllable), /ĭ//n/-/s//ī//d/ – *in-side* (2 vowel sounds, 2 syllables)
- affixes (prefixes, suffixes) are syllables (***pre****-school, dark-**ness***) – separating these aids in fluency and comprehension
- compound words are divided between words (*wrist-watch, tooth-brush, bare-foot*)
- consonant digraphs (*sh, th, ch*) are kept together (*wor-ship, fea-ther, me-chan-ic*)
- when two or more consonants appear in the middle of the word, divide between them (*pic-nic, dol-lar, den-tist*) – this assists in knowing the vowel sound
- in Chapter 3 – Vowels, we discussed the schwa sound (/uh/) in the unstressed syllable. In syllabication, understanding the role the schwa sound plays becomes important because we may be able to predict how to divide the word based on vowel sounds but be unsure of the vowel to write in that syllable (*ball**a**oon, wisd**o**m, sof**a**, ribb**o**n, supp**o**rt*).

Margaret Stanbuck, an educator and researcher interested in refining instruction for dyslexic students conducted a study of a frequency-based list of 17,602 words (1992). Her goal was to discern the consistency of vowels in syllables, particularly those with rimes (see Chapter 5 for information about rimes). In the following six syllable descriptions, Stanbuck's percentage of consistency is given. Overall, she found rimes were highly useful in teaching about syllables to assist reading. A summary of the types and general rules about syllables are summarized in Appendix D.

The six types of syllables are:

1. **closed**
    - this dependable syllable ends with a consonant and the vowel is short
    - this is usually the first syllable taught because it is the most common
    - this syllable appears in rimes, making the vowel sound stable
    - Stanbuck found rimes have a predictability of 95% for short vowels
    - Examples:

r***ug***	lap-t***op***
j***ump***	live-***stock***
sl***ick***	***scrap***-book
s***at***	rab-***bit***

Syllables

2. **open**
   - this syllable ends in a vowel and the vowel sound is long
   - Stanback found the long sound predictable for *e, o,* and *u* 90% of the time for this type of syllable
   - Examples:

m**e**	b**a**-by
fl**y**	v**e**-to
g**o**	p**a**-per
fl**u**	t**i**-ger

3. **vowel-consonant-silent e**
   - in this syllable the vowel is generally long (we already know the rule about words like *have*)
   - this pattern is typically found at the end of a word
   - Stanbuck found variation in the consistency of the vowel being long. The VC*e* combinations and percentages of dependability are:
     - a_e – 70% (*bake, made, trace*)
     - e_e – 76% (*these, scene, convene*)
     - i_e – 62% (*dime, rice, vine*)
     - o_e – 81% (*bone, home, spoke*)
     - u_e – 69% (*use, cube, huge*)
     - y_e – 100% (*type, style, thyme*)

     a. Examples:

n**a**me	de-b**a**te
g**e**ne	in-ter-v**e**ne
s**i**de	pro-v**i**de
p**o**le	dis-cl**o**se
b**y**te	kil-o-byte

4. **vowel team and diphthong**
    - in this syllable two or more vowels come together to make one sound
    - the vowels stay together in the syllable with a 90% occurrence, according to Stanbuck
    - Examples:

b**oa**t	c**au**-tion
b**oi**l	dis-c**ou**nt
sp**oo**n	p**oi**-son
t**ee**th	be-tw**ee**n

5. *r*-controlled
    - when *r* marks a vowel, it stays in the syllable with the vowel
    - Stanbuck found the consistency varied with the pronunciation of the vowels in the *r*-controlled syllables: /är/ at 56%, /ôr/ at 62%, and /ûr/ spelled *er* at 93%, *ir* at 70%, and *ur* at 99%
    - While the *r* always remains with the vowel, the vowel sound may change depending on where it is in the word (*stir* versus *miracle*)
    - Examples:

f**ir**st	n**or**-mal
p**ar**k	t**ur**-tle
t**ur**n	th**ir**-sty
b**or**n	p**er**-form

6. **consonant – le**
    - This syllable is a consonant followed by the letters *le* and is usually found at the end of a word
    - These are always multisyllabic words

Syllables

- Stanbuck found consistency 100% of the time for this syllable type
- Examples:

ta-**ble**	ap-**ple**
puz-**zle**	wig-**gle**
han-**dle**	stum-**ble**
bub-**ble**	lit-**tle**

Examining this last syllable type (consonant – le) might make us wonder about similar sounding, but differently spelled endings: *-el* and *-al*. Some guidelines for choosing *-le*, *-el*, or *-al* are:

- *– le* is used most often and follows eleven of the consonants:

Consonant	Example
b	trouble, table
c	cycle, muscle
ck	trickle, freckle
d	handle, noodle
f	rifle, waffle
g	bugle, eagle
k	twinkle, wrinkle
p	simple, maple
st	whistle, castle
t	settle, title
z	puzzle, sizzle

- a hint is to consider the "look" of the consonant that precedes *-le*. The letters *b, d, f, k (ck)*, and *t (st)* are printed with "tall" parts before the *-le* (called "sticks" when teaching handwriting). The letters *g* and *p* are printed with parts that drop below the line (called "tails"). Words with a "stick" or "tail" generally use *-le*.

Letters with "Sticks" (b, d, f, k, l, t) Using -le	Letters with "Tails" (g, p) Using -le
b – table, double	g – wiggle, eagle
d – fiddle, noodle	p – apple, maple
f – rifle, waffle	
k and ck – ankle, twinkle, tackle, pickle	
t and st – cattle, shuttle, castle, hustle	

- The letters *m, n, r, v, w* do not have a stick or tail. These words generally end in either *-el* or *-al*. There is no hard and fast rule for *-el* versus *-al* (except when *-al* is used as a suffix), so we must rely on our B.E.E. when writing.

Consonants m, n, r, v, w Followed by -el	Consonants m, n, r, v, w Followed by -al
m – camel, caramel	m – animal, normal
n – tunnel, panel	n – final, signal
r – quarrel, barrel	r – coral, rural
v – level, novel	v – oval, rival
w – vowel, jewel	w – narwal (there are very few -wal words)

- *–al* is the suffix added to words to show qualities or actions – *bride/bridal, magic/magical, comic/comical, tide/tidal, renew/renewal, globe/global, arrive/arrival, center/central*

APPLICATION ROUTINES IN ACTION

Now that we have examined the six syllable types, ask students to apply what they have learned using the Application Routines. You will want to adjust for your population, perhaps choosing different syllable types or words, but these three examples will get you started in planning following syllable instruction.

Application Routine Showcase: Find It with Open Syllables

Invite students to hunt for examples of words with syllables that end in a long vowel sound (open syllable). Ask students to use a content book and its glossary (if they want) for the hunt. Give them the following directions:

Syllables

*Use your Social Studies or Mathematics book to hunt for words with open syllables that end in a long vowel sound. For instance, in the first syllable, the word **crisis** has a long i sound and **equation** has a long e sound. Remember, you will be looking for multisyllabic words with an open syllable and long vowel sound. When you find a word, write it on your collection sheet. Be ready to share your findings!*

Application Routine Showcase: Remember It with Compound Words

Create word cards that break compound words into syllables: *cook-book, pan-cake, dog-house, ear-ring, some-thing, tooth-pick, wheel-chair, star-fish.* Spread the cards out, face down where all students can see them. Taking turns, have students turn two cards over. If the match makes a compound word, they keep the pair. Otherwise, they turn them face down and the next player tries to make a match. Once all the matches are made, have students who have a set of cards work with a buddy to think of other compound words with either of those words. For instance, the student who has *something* might list *someone, sometime, somehow, someday, some-

body, anything, everything, nothing.* The students with *pancake* might list *cupcake, hotcake, cakewalk, teacake, dishpan, dustpan.* To offer more support, the two parts of each compound word can be written on different color cards. This narrows the options for making matches.

Application Routine Showcase: Sort It with a Closed Sort of Number of Syllables

Create a closed sort by making the following key word cards: *1 syllable, 2 syllables, 3 syllables.* Then make word cards: *frame, place, slant, splotch, preview, fraction, planet, spelling, president, peppermint, transmitter, magician.* Place the three key words in different locations in the classroom. Pass the word cards to buddies. Ask them to say the word softly to themselves and think about how many syllables they hear. As students to go the spot that has the number of syllables in their word, invite them to check each other's words for accuracy (buddies can "advise" others to relocate, if needed). Ask each group to create a list of six more words with the same number of syllables as their words have and then share their sorted words and the ones they thought of that fit that category. Have the group write each of their new words on a card. This Routine can then be moved to side work or small group as a review of sorting the syllables, using more words.

CHAPTER SUMMARY

Once secure in their knowledge of consonant and vowel sounds, teaching students to be aware of syllables helps with decoding and encoding fluency. Helping them understand that the number of vowel sounds we hear defines the number of syllables in a word is an important concept to apply to multisyllabic words. The six types of syllables were defined, and example words were given for each. Breaking a word into syllables assists the reader in decoding new words and helps the writer move toward conventional spellings. Syllabication can help a reader approximate the pronunciation of a word, thus aiding in comprehension.

Further Reading

Jennifer Diliberto's study of systematic, direct instruction in syllables found struggling readers could make gains in word attack and reading comprehension.
   Diliberto, Jennifer A., John R. Beattie, Claudia P. Flowers, and Robert F. Algozzine. 2008. "Effects of Teaching Syllable Skills Instruction on Reading Achievement in Struggling Middle School Readers." *Literacy Research and Instruction, 48*(1): 14 27. https://doi.org/10.1080/19388070802226253

Researcher Linnea Ehri explains how children retain words and develop orthographic mapping:
   Ehri, Linnea C. 2014. "Orthographic Mapping in the Acquisition of Sight Word Reading, Spelling Memory, and Vocabulary Learning." *Scientific Studies of Reading, 18*(1): 5–21.

Researcher Margaret Stanbuck, an educator interested in helping dyslexic students, analyzed word lists to find the most useful approach for helping her students:
   Stanback, Margaret L. 1992. "Syllable and Rime Patterns for Teaching Reading: Analysis of a Frequency-based Vocabulary of 17,602 Words." *Annals of Dyslexia, 42*: 196–221.

Recognized researcher and distinguished professor, Charles Perfetti's classic article places reading ability and disability on a "continuum that contains a wide range of coding ability" (11). His take on how decoding is learned offers ideas that differentiate student needs:
   Perfetti, Charles A. 1986. "Continuities in Reading Acquisition, Reading Skill and Reading Disability." *RASE, 7*(1): 11–21.

Chapter 7

But Wait! There's More!

When I was having that alphabet soup, I never thought that it would pay off.
– Vanna White, Co-host of *Wheel of Fortune*

This book closes with some additional topics that just need a bit of a spotlight. It is hard to have a serious conversation about phonics without some of these topics sneaking in. How does what we have already examined help us with questions such as:

- Why do we sometimes drop an *e* when adding a suffix, but not always?
- Why (and when) do we double some consonants before adding suffixes?
- Why does *-able* work for some words, but *-ible* on others?
- How do we put our phonic knowledge to work with homonyms (*flour/flower*)?
- Are there some etymologies, or word origins, we should dip into?
- What are the other "nyms" in English?

This chapter will feel a bit different than the others you've read so far. Just like the infomercial ("But Wait, There's More") that told us we couldn't live without that vegetable chopper or the spray that covers bald spots on your head – this chapter has information you must have! This chapter has "more" of the English language you just can't live without!

BUT WAIT! THERE'S MORE ON STRUCTURAL ANALYSIS

Structural analysis breaks words into their meaningful parts. For instance, *changeable* is that airline ticket we are *-able* to *change*. *Jumped* is the past tense (*-ed*) of *jump*. Let's begin with three questions about adding suffixes that structural analysis will help us answer:

- Why do we sometimes we drop an *e* when adding a suffix, but not always?
- How do we know when we use *-able* or *-ible*?
- Why (and when) do we double some consonants before adding suffixes?

Maintaining Rules When Adding Suffixes

Phonics is more than learning the consonant and vowel sounds. It is also about how words are constructed to maintain "rules" we learned about the letters and sounds. Let's consider two words, with a base word that ends in *e* before adding the suffix:

- *replace – replacing*
- *replace – replaceable*

Structural analysis shows us the base word (*replace*) plus a suffix (*-ing, -able*). The *e* dropped before adding *-ing*, but not before *-able*. Why? Think back to the chapter on consonants. We learned that *c* sounds like /k/ when followed by *a, o,* or *u* (*cat, coat, cut*) and /s/ when followed by *e, i,* or *y* (*cent, city, cycle*). If we drop the *e* from *replace*, adding *-able* would give *c* the /k/ sound, changing the pronunciation of the word. With *replacing*, the *i* maintains the /s/ sound of *c*. So, the hard and soft sounds of *c* (and *g*) always get top billing! Here are a few more examples, with *c* and *g* being in charge when adding suffixes – *changeable/changing, chargeable/charging, noticeable/noticing,* and *forceable/forcing*. Since the hard and soft sounds of *c* and *g* are so reliable, helping students remember this rule when adding suffixes can answer a lot of questions about spelling.

Rules for Adding *-able* or *-ible*

When do we pick one or the other – is it *-able* or *-ible*? Look at the words below and notice what the suffix is added to:

But Wait! There's More!

-able	-able	-ible	-ible
dependable	profitable	audible	flexible
breakable	laughable	horrible	edible
perishable	acceptable	legible	credible
workable	comfortable	feasible	visible

In the first two columns, when we remove *-able*, a base word remains: *depend, profit, break, laugh, perish, accept, work,* and *comfort*. In the third and fourth columns, when we remove *-ible*, a root remains: *aud-, flex-, horr-, ed-, leg-, cred-, feas-,* and *vis-*. The rules that generally serve us for choosing *-able* or *-ible* are:

- add *-able* to base words (*spread, accept, enjoy, perish*)
  - about 80% of words with the suffix meaning "capable or worthy of" have this spelling
  - an interesting fact is *-able* is the only spelling of this suffix that can be used when new words are created (*recyclable* – able to recycle, *adorkable* – able to be appealing or cute in an awkward way)
- add *-ible* to (Latin based) root words (*gull-, poss-, plaus-, elig-*)
  - this suffix is never added to newly created words because there are no new Latin words
- drop the *e marker* unless *c* or *g* is before it in the base word (*changeable, noticeable*)
- words ending in *t* change to *ss* and have *-ible* added (*transmit/transmissible*)

Adding -able after	Rule	Example
A base word	No change needed	teachable (teach) lendable (lend)
A base word ending in *e*	Drop *e* marker – suffix maintains long vowel sound	notable (note) usable (use)
A base word, ending in *ce* or *ge*, do not drop *e*	Maintain soft sound of *c* and *g*	noticeable (notice) manageable (manage)
Adding -ible after	**Rule**	**Example**
A root	Add to Latin-based roots	visible (vis-)
A word ending in *t*	*t* changes to *ss*	admissible (admit) permissible (permit)

Of course, English being what it is, some words don't fit these rules, but they do indeed have conventions of their own. Words of Latin origin influence the choice of suffix. These are rare, so if a student tries to include these in their writing, we applaud the effort, whether they spelled it conventionally or not. We can explain to that adventurous writer that the Latin origins of words have such a long history they sometimes do unexpected things! A few of the words we would expect to end in *-able* but do not:

- collapsible (*collapsus* "to fall together")
- contemptible (*contemnere* "to scorn")

A few of the words we would expect to end in *-ible* but do not:

- memorable (*memorabilis* "worthy of being remembered")
- portable (*portabilis* "that can be carried")

Rules for Dropping or Doubling Consonants When Adding Suffixes

Speaking of adding suffixes, why do we double the consonant of some base words? The reason has to do with vowel sounds. Let's look at two easy ones to compare:

- *hoping*
- *hopping*

We can differentiate between these words by seeing that *hoping* required dropping the *e* from *hope* because the *i* in the *-ing* suffix does the job of the *e* to mark the vowel, *o*, long. By doubling the *p* in the word *hop*, we maintain the short *o* vowel sound. In essence, we put a "wall" between the short vowel and the *-ing* suffix to maintain the vowel sound. Here are other word pairs that help clarify the function of doubling the consonant versus dropping the *e* marker:

- *striping* (*stripe* – The road worker was *striping* the turn lanes.); *stripping* (*strip* – The carpenter was *stripping* the old varnish.)
- *taping* (*tape* – She was *taping* the gift wrap.); *tapping* (*tap* – He was *tapping* to the beat of the music.)
- *waging* (*wage* – We were *waging* a bet who could run the fastest.); *wagging* (*wag* – The dog's tail was *wagging*.)

But Wait! There's More!

Of course, some words simply have the suffix added (*sleeping, jumping, holding*) because the *-ing* will not change the vowel sounds (/ē/, /ŭ/, /ō/). The overarching question we want students to ask is, "what should I do when I add a suffix to be sure the vowel sounds the same?"

Adding *-ing*	Rule	Example
Base word ending in *ce*, drop *e*	Suffix helps maintain the long vowel sound and maintains the soft sound of *c*	dancing noticing rejoicing
Base word with short vowel, double the consonant	Extra consonant protects short vowel sound	tripping hopping begging

BUT WAIT! THERE'S MORE ON HOMONYMS

Next, we turn our attention to homonyms. This classification of words is greatly influenced by our eye, ear, and intended word meaning. By using phonic knowledge, reading a homonym is not the problem – we sound across and understand the word in context. The challenge comes in choosing the correct spelling when we write. Is it *their*, *there*, or *they're*? Is it *too*, *to*, or *two*? Homonyms are words with the same oral or written form but different origin and meaning. These words have the same number of vowel sounds (syllables), same number of consonant letter sounds, but context is everything. The two kinds of homonyms are homophones and homographs.

Homophones

These words that have the same (homo) sound (phon) but different spellings and meanings (I will *write* the *right* answer.) Notice that the vowel sound (/ī/) is the same in both words, the consonant sounds are the same (/r/ and /t/), but the spelling and, obviously, the meanings are very different. The tricky bit of this category of words is many computer spell checkers will not pick up on an error. If the writer means *there* and types *their* the computer recognizes the second one as a "real" word and may not flag it. *Our brain and eye must be smarter than the computer!*

Just for Fun

Give students a challenge – can they figure out these homophone riddles? This activity raises their awareness for these types of words. Post one a day, giving them time to think about the answer. Or challenge students to create their own. Here are a few to get you started:

- *What animal lost its voice?* A hoarse horse.
- *What animal lost all its fur?* A bare bear.

- *Who is a man in armor outside in the dark?* A knight in the night.
- *What is a royal chair that was tossed out the window?* A thrown throne.
- *What happened to the amphibian with a broken-down car?* The toad got towed.
- *Who is a deer making bread?* A doe with dough.

Homographs

These words have the same (*homo*) written (*graph*) form but have different meanings.

- The first type of homograph includes words written and pronounced the same but have different meanings:
  - The *bat* hung from the tree. I have a new baseball *bat*.
  - While I sat in the traffic *jam* I ate the jar of strawberry *jam*.
  - She had to *duck* when the *duck* flew over her head.

- The second type of homograph is referred to as **a heteronym** (*hetero* – different, *nym* – name). These words have the same spelling, but different pronunciations and meanings:
  - The *tear* in her dress brought a *tear* to her eye.
  - The gauze was *wound* around the *wound*.
  - In single-syllable words the vowel sound changes: I took the *lead* (/ē/) since Nancy *lead* (/ĕ/) the lunch line yesterday.
  - In multisyllabic words a heteronym occurs when we shift the accented syllable: **con**´-tent (happy), con-**tent**´ (topics); de-**sert**´ (leave), **de**´-sert – (arid land).

Anticipated Misunderstandings

Homophones create issues for writers. While we can easily read *there, their,* and *they're*, writing them correctly is sometimes a challenge. In this category of words, we can use our ear from our B.E.E. (Brain, Ear, Eye), but need our eye to determine if we have chosen wisely. Helping students think about the context and the meaning they intend is key to conventionalizing spellings such as these. Look for fun and engaging ways to help their brains and eyes see the differences in these words more clearly. For instance, you might share this trick with them – *there* contains the word *here* – so it refers to a place, *their* contains the letter *i* so has to do with a person, and *they're* is the contraction of *they are*. Or, challenge them to think of spellings for homophones to raise their awareness of the words. Which ones have two spellings (plane, plain; waist, waste), three spellings (do, dew, due; to, two, too) and four spellings (carrot, karat, carat, caret)?

BUT WAIT! THERE'S MORE ON WORD ORIGINS

Throughout this book there have been references to the history of English and how that influences phonics, spellings, and pronunciations. The beginning of Chapter 1 quoted Eliza Naumann from *Bee Season*. Eliza wins a spelling bee, much to her father's surprise. She shares, "My father told me once that words and letters hold all the secrets of the universe, that in their shape and sounds I could find anything."

The history of the English language does, indeed, have secrets we need to tell. There is much to know about the history of the English language. It's a story of invaders, settlers, and marriages – and how Jacob Grimm (of the Grimm Brothers fame) figured out how it was all connected. Suffice to say, sometimes, when a student wonders why a word it spelled as it is, the etymology (or word origin) might give us the answer. And we help them create memories about words, rather than memorize (with perhaps short-term consequences). For example, *easel* comes from the Dutch word *ezel* meaning "donkey." This "beast of burden" was created by Dutch artists for the name of the stand they created to hold a canvas (they also gave us "landscape"). Appendix E provides a listing of interesting word origin stories from across the curriculum to share with students.

Just for Fun

After the class has been working with word origins, a fun review game is "I am, who is?" This is a chain activity. Create the chain the first time the students play, using word origins they have been studying. Each strip asks the question "who is?" The next strip in the chain answers, "I am" and then asks for the next "who is." The first strip begins, "I am the first word tracker. Who is . . ." The last strip ends with "I am the last word tracker. Who is the first word tracker?" After making the strips, cut them apart and distribute to students. To engage a larger group, once a student reads their strip they pass it to someone who does not have one. You can circle around the strips as many times as you wish, providing opportunity for a deeper review. For example (see Appendix E for each word origin story):

I am the first word tracker. Who is the Latin word meaning "to force apart?"

I am *divide*. Who is the Greek word meaning "having long hair?"

I am *comet*. Who is the Irish Gaelic word meaning "enough or plenty?"

I am *galore*. Who is the Latin word meaning "person dressed in white?"

I am *candidate*. Who is the Anglo-French word meaning "a breaking?"

I am *fraction*. Who is the Latin word meaning "little mouse?"

I am *muscle*. Who is the Proto-Germanic word meaning "two left over ten?"

I am *twelve* **and I am the last word tracker. Who is the first word tracker?**

You can also create multiple sets and break students into small groups or create longer chains by using more word origins. Once students are familiar with the activity, organize small groups to work together to create chains. Groups cut apart, then swap their chains with another group. These can also be used for side work. The strips are shuffled and then students put them in the correct order.

BUT WAIT! THERE'S MORE ON THE REST OF THE "NYMS"

There are more members of the "nym" family besides homonyms – acronyms, antonyms, eponyms, retronyms, and synonyms. Taking these words apart (using structural analysis) makes their meanings clear (-*nym* means "name" in all of the following examples).

Acronyms

Acro means "high." The "high" (or first) letter of each word is used. Some familiar acronyms:

- *ZIP* (Zone Improvement Plan)
- *NASA* (National Aeronautics and Space Administration)
- *PIN* (Personal Identification Number)
- *EPCOT* (Experimental Prototype Community of Tomorrow)
- *ATM* (Automated Teller Machine)

Antonyms

Anti means "opposite." Some are easy opposites – big, small. But we can add shades of meaning when working with these – how big? Large? Huge? Enormous? How small? Tiny? Teensy? Minute (there's one of those heteronyms)?

Eponyms

Epo means "called after" (words that originate from people's names). Here are a few fun ones:

- *Graham cracker* – 19th-century minister, Sylvester Graham, advocated for healthy living. He ground coarse wheat flour and created a cracker he promoted as a wholesome option for his vegetarian diet.
- *Fahrenheit* – In 1714, Prussian physicist Gabriel D. Fahrenheit invented the mercury thermometer and the temperature scale that is still used today. His experiments with freezing and boiling points produced a scale of numbers that could be measured by the expansion of mercury in a glass tube.

But Wait! There's More!

- *Frisbee* – the Frisbie Bakery in Bridgeport, Connecticut, sold pies to Yale students. The pies came in metal pans and for fun, the students would toss empty pans to each other. In the 1950s, Wham-O toy company got the idea to make the plastic Frisbee.

Retronyms

Retro means "back." These are words created due to an invention or change over time. The word has been "back named" to account for these changes. For instance, we use to say *mail* but now need *e-mail* and *snail mail*. Here a few more:

- *World War I* was called the *Great War* until we entered *World War II*
- *cloth diaper* after *disposable diapers* were invented
- *hardwired* after some products became *wireless*
- *whole milk* after the introduction of *2%, low-fat,* and *skim milk*
- *corn on the cob* once *canned corn* became available.

Synonyms

Syn means "same." These words have the same meaning, such as *ask* and *question.* Students sometimes go the thesaurus, looking for a synonym to jazz up their writing. Of course, that sometimes leads us down the wrong path. A classic episode of the television show *Friends* ("The One Where Rachel's Sister Babysits") demonstrates the folly in sometimes using a thesaurus. Joey writes a letter of reference about his friends: "They're humid prepossessing homo sapiens with full-sized aortic pumps" ("They're warm, nice people with big hearts."). He meant well. Synonym work does give you a window into students' vocabulary, so asking them to switch out words in their writing engages them in synonym work.

APPLICATION ROUTINES IN ACTION

We close out this chapter (and this book) with a few more Application Routines in action. These three examples look at ways to apply developing knowledge about word origins, doubling a consonant or dropping an *e* before adding a suffix, and choosing *-able* or *-ible*.

Application Routine Showcase: Remember It with Word Origins

Have students involved in making the cards for this Routine. Give students a list of words (perhaps related to content studies) and ask them to work together to investigate the word origins using etymonline.com. This useful resource provides the origins of words, how they might have sounded in their original language, and their definition (especially how it might have evolved over time). For instance, words from Mathematics: *equation, divide, eleven, fraction, multiply, perimeter, twelve, zero* (See Appendix E for information on these words). Have students create the "Remember It" cards by writing, on three differently colored cards, (1) the word, (2) its origin story, and (3) its meaning (e.g., (1) *zero*, (2) Arabic word meaning "empty place," (3) a number with no quantity). Or, for students up to the challenge, ask them to find eight words of interest related to a particular topic (solar system, renewable energy). After they have created the card sets with words, origins, and meanings, spread them out with the word face up. Turn the origin story and meaning cards face down. Students take turns trying to match the three parts. When they find the story and/or meaning match, they place it with the word. Play continues until they have matched all the words with their origin and meaning cards.

Application Routine Showcase: Find It for Words with Doubled Consonant or Dropped *e*

Give students two categories of words to find in a text of your choice (free reading or content text): *Words with a doubled consonant before adding a suffix* and *Words with final e dropped before adding a suffix*. As they look through their texts ask them to record their findings on a collection sheet.

Application Showcase Routine: Build It with *-able* and *-ible*

Give students base and root word cards to build words with an *-able* or *-ible* suffix. Make these base and root cards: *depend, profit, accept, comfort, flex, cred, vis, leg*. Make four each of the suffixes *-able* and *-ible*. Have students spread the base, root, and suffix cards out. Ask them to build words with the correct suffix. If they are doing this as side work, ask the students to record the words they made on a collection sheet.

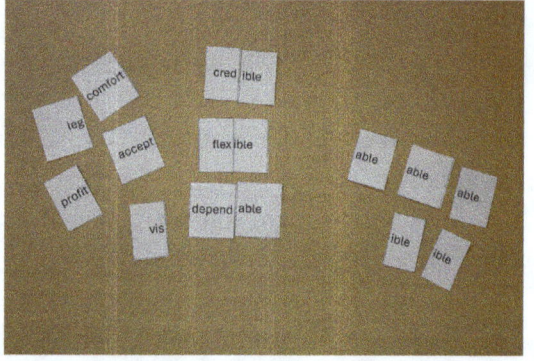

CHAPTER SUMMARY

In this final chapter the threads of learning phonics were woven into the bigger picture of more complex words. The rules of phonics guide us in structural analysis and provide guidance in how to add suffixes. Homonyms are easy to read (*there, their, they're*), but it's sometimes a challenge to predict the correct spelling when writing them. Application of phonic rules makes us stronger readers and writers. And there is a fun factor to learning about English. Word origins not only can explain why a word is spelled as it is but also offers a memorable story that may help orthographically map letters and sounds (and meanings!). If you are not quite done learning about the

But Wait! There's More!

Proto-Indo-European to Modern English journey, Bill Bryson is an engaging author who explores its history in two readable (and entertaining) books: *The Mother Tongue: English and How It Got That Way* (1990) and *Made in America: An Informal History of the English Language in the United States* (2013).

But this end is only the beginning. My intention throughout this book has been to lead you with helpful information about phonics and replicable Application Routines that will support you as you meet the needs of the learners with whom you work and help to develop their knowledge. I hope the information has moved you to pause and reflect on your knowledge base and your efforts to make those you instruct become successful readers and writers. Thank you for journeying along with me in this phonics handbook! My desire is that it has made you and your students feel more confident in the beautiful ways of phonics and the English language.

Further Reading

For lessons to expand vocabulary through work with "nyms," similes, metaphors, idioms, and word origins:
Fresch, Mary Jo, and David L. Harrison. 2020. *Empowering Students' Knowledge of Vocabulary: Learning How Language Works, Grades 3–5.* Champaign, IL: National Council of Teachers of English.

For guidance in teaching multilingual learners about homonyms, homophones, and homographs, a school-based educator and two literacy professors teamed up to create a suggested instructional process:
Jacobson, Julie, Diane Lapp, and James Flood. 2007. "A Seven-step Instructional Plan for Teaching English-language Learners to Comprehend and Use Homonyms, Homophones, and Homographs." *Journal of Adolescent & Adult Literacy, 511* (2): 98–111. https://doi.org/10.1598/JAAL.51.2.2

These authors (a researcher and classroom teacher) spent time researching how to best teach the spelling patterns of English. Their years of classroom-based work suggests an approach that is child-centered and improves students' knowledge of phonics:
Fresch, Mary Jo, and Aileen Wheaton. 2002. *Teaching and Assessing Spelling: A Practical Approach That Strikes the Balance between Whole-Group and Individualized Instruction.* Amazon Books.

Appendix A: How Consonants Are Articulated

Classification	How the Mouth Articulates the Sound	Consonants	Examples
Plosives (Also called Stops)	• The air flow is blocked as the sound is made • Place of air block can be: – lips (b, p) – behind the teeth (d, t) – back of throat (g, k) • Sounding the consonant creates a puff of air	b p d t g k	bat pat dot tot got, ghost kit (cat, chaos)
Fricatives	• These sounds are made by forcing a continuous stream of air through a narrow space • The narrow space is created by: – placing the teeth on lip (v, f) – the tongue between teeth (th) – at the ridge behind teeth (z, s) – on the roof of mouth (ch, sh, zh)	f v th (unvoiced) th (voiced) s (unvoiced) z (voiced) sh zh	fat (phone) vat thank this sat (cent, city) zoo shop, chef pleasure
Affricates	• These sounds are a combination Stop and Fricative • Sounds are created by stopping air flow and then immediately releasing it	j (voiced) ch (unvoiced)	jump (gem, giant, cage, dodge) chain, match

Copyright material from Mary Jo Fresch (2026), *The Phonics Handbook*, Routledge.

(Continued)

Classification	How the Mouth Articulates the Sound	Consonants	Examples
Nasals	• These sounds are made by closing the mouth and forcing the air through the nose by:		
	– closing the lips (m)	m	man (calm, limb, autumn)
	– using the ridge behind the teeth (n)	n	nice, sign, gnat, knock
	– using the back of the throat (ng)	ng	sing (tank)
Liquids	• These sounds are formed by slightly interrupting the airflow with no friction	l r	loud run (wrote, rhyme)
Glides	• These sounds glide right into the vowel that follows it and are sounded at:		
	– roof of mouth (y)	y	yell
	– back of throat (wh/hw)	wh/hw	who, what
	– in throat (h)	h	ham

Appendix B: Consonants

Consonant	Dependability	Descriptions	Examples
b	Consistent sound /b/ at the beginning of a word	• Voiced consonant • Silent after m • Silent before t	*boy* *comb* *debt*
d	Consistent /d/ sound	• Voiced consonant	*day*
f	Consistent /f/ sound	• Unvoiced consonant	*fan*
g	70% hard sound (/guh/) 29% soft sound (/j/) 1% silent	• Voiced consonant • Hard sound (/guh/) when followed by a, o, u • Soft sound (/j/) when followed by e, i, y • Silent when precedes n	*gate, goat, gush* *gentle, giant, gym* *gnaw*
h	99% consistent in /h/ sound	• Never final sound of a word • Silent in borrowed French words • Silent when following g or r	*hat* *honor* *ghost, rhyme*
j	100% consistent in /j/ sound at beginning of word	• Never the letter that represents the final /j/ sound	*jump*
k	Consistent in /k/ sound Silent .5% when followed by n	• Unvoiced consonant • Could replace c (which sounds like /k/ 76% of the time) • Silent when followed by n	*kale* *candy* *knee*

Copyright material from Mary Jo Fresch (2026), *The Phonics Handbook*, Routledge.

(Continued)

Consonant	Dependability	Descriptions	Examples
l	Consistent in /l/ sound	• Silent before final k after a and o • Pronounced before final k following i	last talk, yolk milk
m	Consistent in /m/ sound	Makes no other sound	man
n	Consistent in /n/ sound	• Makes no other sound • Silent following m • Shifts to back of throat when followed by g or k	name autumn ring sink
p	Consistent in /p/ sound	• Unvoiced consonant • When written with h (ph) makes /f/ sound	page phone
r	Consistent in /r/ sound	• Makes no other sound • When follows a vowel the r influences the vowel sound	ray car, perk, bird, fork, curb
s	84% consistent in /s/ sound 12% of the time takes on /zh/ and /sh/ sounds	• Unvoiced consonant • Marks plurals	sand treasure, sugar jobs
t	98% consistent in /t/ sound	• Unvoiced consonant • Silent if follows f • Silent if follows s, unless a blend	tale soften castle
v	100% consistent in /v/ sound	• Voiced consonant • Makes no other sound • No English words end in v	vest
w	Consistent /w/ sound at beginning of word when followed by vowel	• Represents vowel when teamed with a, e, o • Silent when precedes r	wave claw, flew, snow write

y	100% consistent /y/ sound at beginning of word or syllable, the only time it is a consonant	• Has three vowel sounds
		  – long i
		  – short i
		  – long e
			yam
			cry
			myth
			baby
			can-yon

Copyright material from Mary Jo Fresch (2026), *The Phonics Handbook*, Routledge.

Appendix B

(Continued)

Consonant	Dependability	Descriptions	Examples
th	Most frequent digraph	• Can be voiced or unvoiced • Unvoiced 100% of the time when follows a consonant	that thing month
sh	Second most occurring digraph Consistent and reliable in sound	• Can occur at beginning or end of word	sheep wash
ch	89% sounds like /ch/ as in *chair* 10% sounds like /k/ as in *chaos* 1% sounds like /sh/ as in *chef*	• Sound differences due to language of origin • /ch/ Old or Middle English words • /k/ Greek words • /sh/ French words • Written as *tch* when ending a short vowel word • Written as *ch* when ending a long vowel word with a 100% occurrence	chair chaos chef match peach
ng/nk	100% consistency in /ng/ sound at end of word	• Never appears at beginning of a word • At end of word when spelled nk blends with the k	ring sink
wh (/hw/)	90% of the time makes /hw/ sound at beginning of word 10% of the time makes /wh/ sound	• Never the final sound of a word	wheel what
ph	Consistent /f/ sound at the beginning, medial, and final sounds of words	• Occurring less often in early literacy words	phone alphabet lymph
gh	Combined with ou makes two sounds	• One sound of ough is /off/ sound • Second sound of ough is /aw/ sound • Silent in some words and makes vowel long	cough thought dough

Copyright material from Mary Jo Fresch (2026), *The Phonics Handbook*, Routledge.

(Continued)

Consonant	Dependability	Descriptions	Examples
S family blends	st, sp, sc, sk, sl, sw, sn, sm	• High degree of consistency in the s family blends • Sk and st can be at end of words and make the same sounds in either position	stir, space, scan, skim, slam, swan, snag, small desk, best
R family blends	pr, tr, gr, br, cr, dr, fr	• High degree of consistency in the r family blends	prize, trip, grin, brag, crowd, drop, from
L family blends	pl, cl, bl, fl, gl	• High degree of consistency in the l family blends	plan, clap, blank, flew, glue
tw blend		• High degree of consistency • At the beginning of words or syllables	twin be-tween
thr	Th plus r blended	• Only at the beginning of words	three
shr	Sh plus r blended	• Only at the beginning of words	shred
spr, spl, squ, str, scr	These blends are consistent in sound	• Only at the beginning of words	spring, splash, squish, string, scrub
Ending blends	ct, ft, ld, lf, lp, lt, mp, nd, nk, nt, pt, rd, sp	• Consistent blending sounds	fact, left, fold, golf, help, melt, jump, send, link, sent, kept, word, wasp
Silent patterns	tch, dg, wr, kn, gn, bm, lk, ps, wh, bt, gh, mn	• When these letters are combined one letter is generally silent (see lk and wh for other sounds)	match, dodge, write, knee, gnat, lamb, talk, psychic, whose, debt, ghost, column

Copyright material from Mary Jo Fresch (2026), *The Phonics Handbook*, Routledge.

Appendix C: Vowels

Vowel	Spellings	Descriptions	Examples
/ă/	a	• Short a is dependable in sound when between two consonants	apple cat, map demand
/ĕ/	e ea	• The two spellings of the short e sound are e and ea • The ea spelling is the only vowel team with a short sound	bed head
/ĭ/	i y	• The two spellings of the short i sound are i and y • Y spellings are usually Greek words • English words do not end in i	ink myth, oxygen
/ŏ/	o wa qua	• The three spellings of the short o sound are o, wa, qua • O is short when between two consonants • Wa and qu make the a sound like short o	odd dog, coffee watch, wand quality, squad
/ŭ/	u o	• The two spellings of the short u sound are u and o • U is short between two consonants • English words do not end in u	up love, tough fun
/ā/	a a_e ai ay (ee, ea, eigh)	• Long a has the highest number of different spellings: • four most often found are a, a_e, ai, ay • three less common are ee, ea, eigh • A at the end of open syllable is long	cake, rain, day matinee, steak, eight pa-per

Copyright material from Mary Jo Fresch (2026), *The Phonics Handbook*, Routledge.

(Continued)

Vowel	Spellings	Descriptions	Examples
/ē/	e ee, e_e, ea y (ei)	• Long e has five common spellings (e, ee, e_e, ea, y) • The y spelling is at the end of a word • There is one less common spelling (ei) • E at the end of open syllable is long	feet, these, eat, baby city receive ce-dar
/ī/	i y i_e ight, ie	• Long i has five common spellings (i, y, i_e, ight, ie) • I at end of open syllable is long • English words do not end in i	iris, fly, ride, light, pie i-vy
/ō/	o o_e ow	• Long o has three common spellings (o, o_e, ow) • O at end of open syllable is long	open, bone, snow o-boe
/ū/	u u_e ue ew	• Long u has four common spellings (u, u_e, ue, ew) • U at end of open syllable is long • Few English words end in u	use, cube, true, few cu-bic you
/är/	ar	• The ar spelling is usually the first r-controlled vowel taught as it has 89% utility • Has a distinct sound from the other r-controlled vowels	car park
/ôr/	or ore oor oar	• The or spelling is usually the next r-controlled vowel taught • Has a distinct sound from the other r-controlled vowels • There are four spellings of the or sound (or, ore, oor, oar) • It may appear at end of nouns and verbs	corn chore, floor, soar author, neighbor censor, honor
/ûr/	er ur ir	• There are three spellings for the ur sound (er, ur, ir) • Are often difficult to auditorily identify • Er most common spelling and is often added to Old English words for noun meaning "person who has to do with" • Er added to comparative words	her, hurt, dirt teacher, worker taller

Copyright material from Mary Jo Fresch (2026), *The Phonics Handbook*, Routledge.

Appendix C

(Continued)

Vowel	Spellings	Descriptions	Examples
/ow/	ou ow	• The ou diphthong spelling tends to be inside a word or syllable • The ow spelling that sounds like /ow/ tends to be at the end of words	sound cow
/oi/	oi oy	• The oi diphthong spelling occurs at beginning or middle of words, but not at the end • The oy spelling usually occurs in the middle or end of a word	oil, boiler royal, toy
/ə/	any of the five vowels	• The schwa sound is the vowel sound in an unstressed syllable • Can be spelled with any of the vowels • Makes the /uh/ sound regardless of the vowel	**a**go it**e**m fam**i**ly **o**ven **u**pon
/aw/	au aw	• The au digraph spelling tends to be in the beginning or middle of words • The aw digraph spelling is usually at the end of words, especially before the letters l and n	author, sauce claw crawl, lawn
/o͞o/	oo	• One of two sounds for this digraph spelling • Sound difference related to word origin • Classified as "long vowel sound of oo" • Appears at end or within a root	moo spoon mood
/o͝o/	oo	• One of two sounds for this digraph spelling • Sound difference related to word origin • Classified as "short vowel sound of oo" • Similar in sound to short u • Appears within a root especially before k	good book, cook

Copyright material from Mary Jo Fresch (2026), *The Phonics Handbook*, Routledge.

Appendix D: Syllables

Syllable Type	Definition	Description	Examples
Closed	This syllable ends with a consonant and contains a short vowel sound	• A closed syllable has a 95% predictability for having a short vowel sound • It is a stable syllable when part of a rime family.	rug rab-bit cap clock
Open	This syllable ends with vowel and the vowel sound is long	• 90% of the time the e, o, and u at the end of an open syllable will be the long sound	me ve-to
Vowel-consonant-silent e	This syllable generally has a long vowel sound The VCe is often found at end of word	• Often called silent e or e marker words • Does not apply to Vowel-v-silent e, as no English words end in v (historically, e was added)	name de-bate com-pete love, give
Vowel team and diphthong	This syllable has two or more vowels that come together to make one sound The vowel teams and diphthongs are kept together in the syllable	• These syllables include short vowel, long vowel, or diphthong sounds	boat cau-tion poi-son
R-controlled	When r marks a vowel, it stays with the vowel in the syllable	• R controls the vowel sound • The r and the vowel it follows are never separated when breaking a word into syllables	first nor-mal per-fect

(Continued)

Syllable Type	Definition	Description	Examples
Consonant -le	This is a final syllable in a word. The syllable is composed of a consonant followed by the letters *le*.	• This pattern, consonant_le, are always multisyllabic words	ta-ble bea-gle lit-tle

GENERAL RULES ABOUT SYLLABLES

Syllable Rules	Example
Counting vowel sounds identifies the number of syllables in a word. A syllable will have only one vowel sound (which may be represented by more than one vowel letter such as oa for /ō/).	1 vowel sound, 1 syllable – boat – /b//ō//t/ 2 vowel sounds, 2 syllables – in-side – /ĭ//n/-/s//ĭ//d/ 3 vowel sounds, 3 syllables – le-ga-lize – /l//ē/-/g//ə//-/l//ī//z/
Affixes (prefixes, suffixes) are stand-alone syllables, containing one vowel sound.	**pre**-school dark-**ness**
Compound words are divided between whole words to identify the syllables.	wrist-watch tooth-brush bare-foot
Consonant digraphs (*sh, th, ch*) within words are kept together (fea-ther) unless part of a compound word (pot-hole) or prefix (mis-hap).	wor-ship fea-ther me-chan-ic
When two or more consonants appear in the middle of the word, divide between them to identify the syllables.	pic-nic dol-lar den-tist chest-nut tan-trum
The schwa sound (/uh/) is the vowel sound in the unstressed syllable. The sound can be made by any of the vowel letters.	b**a**lloon wisd**o**m sof**a** ribb**o**n

Copyright material from Mary Jo Fresch (2026), *The Phonics Handbook*, Routledge.

Appendix E: Word Origins

This collection is a starting point of vocabulary found in many primary and upper elementary curriculums. On page 85 in Chapter 7, the development of the English language was briefly mentioned. The following words are examples of that long history. This list can be copied and cut apart for a "Match it" activity. As students become involved in researching these, ask them for suggestions of words to add (for instance, after learning about *basketball* they may want to add other sports words such as *soccer* [which is an abbreviation for *association*] or *golf* [Scottish *gouf* meaning "stick, club"). The choices are limitless!

Word	Origin Information
basketball	Invented in 1891 by Canadian Dr. James Naismith, a physical education teacher at International Young Men's Christian Training College in Springfield, Massachusetts. To keep the young men busy during the winter months, he cut the bottoms out of peach baskets and challenged them to move a ball down the gym floor and throw it through the basket.
berserk	Icelandic equivalent of *"savage Norse warrior,"* who wore a coat or shirt of bear fur into battle (and was probably pretty scary looking).
blimp	Floating balloons were classified as rigid and non-rigid. In the early 1900s, the English were attempting to invent a better non-rigid balloon used for military and civilian purposes (travel, weather surveillance). The alphabet was used to name the test models. The first limp (or non-rigid), called plan A, was unsuccessful. The second attempt (*B-limp*) was successful.
candidate	Latin *candidatus* meaning "person dressed in white." Early Roman politicians wore white togas to make a good impression.
caravan	Persian – from *karwan* meaning "company of travelers."
comet	Ancient Greek *kometes* meaning "having long hair." Aristotle first used *kometes* to describe the heavenly body that seems to have long hair trailing from its "head." The name was later adopted into Latin as *cometes*, which eventually made its way to English.

Copyright material from Mary Jo Fresch (2026), *The Phonics Handbook*, Routledge.

(Continued)

Word	Origin Information
curriculum	Latin *curriculum* meaning "a running course" (also a fast chariot).
dandelion	Latin *dens* meaning "teeth" and *leonis* meaning "lion" because the leaf resembles a lion's teeth (this word is related to *dentist, dental*, and *indent*).
disaster	Greek *dis* meaning "bad" or "ill" and *astron* meaning "star." A disaster was considered being under "a bad star."
divide	Latin *dividere* meaning "to force apart."
dumbbell	Bell ringing was quite an art during the Middle Ages. But, just like any instrument that is being learned, novice bellringers practiced for hours and not all of it sounded good! So, a craftsman invented "dumb" or silent bells, which were weighted ropes that did not make noise. The weights of the ropes varied, just as the weights of bells did, so novices got stronger practicing on these.
earmark	Old English herdsmen needed a way to mark their cattle (branding was not yet used). They notched the ears of cattle to signify which was theirs when using common pastureland for grazing.
equation	French *équation* meaning "action of making equal."
eleven	Proto-Germanic *ainlif*, a compound of *ain* meaning "one" plus *leikw* "to leave." To Old English *enleofan* meaning "one left over ten."
Ferris Wheel	George Washington Gale Ferris Jr., an American bridge builder, planned and built the first wheel as a monument for the World's Columbian Exposition in Chicago in 1893.
Fibonacci Sequence	Named for Leonardo Fibonacci, a Tuscan mathematician who discovered the series of numbers in which each is equal to the sum of the preceding two numbers. (0, 1, 1, 2, 3, 5, etc.) This sequence is seen in nature – sunflower heads, pinecones, seashells, flower petals – also called the Golden Ratio.
flu	Shortened form of *influenza*, from Middle Latin *influential* meaning "flow from the heavens." In the 1700s, epidemics were thought to be influenced by the stars.
fraction	Anglo-French *fraccioun* meaning "a breaking."
funny bone	This spot, that gets a "tingly" feeling when bumped, is at the enlarged end of the "humerus" bone.
galore	Irish Gaelic *go leor* meaning "enough or plenty."
globe	Old French *globe* or Latin *globus* meaning "to roll together or stick." At one time maps were only flat and thus rolled together.
hurricane	Taino *huraca'n* meaning "center of the wind." Christopher Columbus brought this word back, making its way to Spanish and eventually English.
jeep	Abbreviation for the all-purpose vehicle developed for the military. The "General Purpose" vehicle became nicknamed *g.p.*, which was shortened into a pronounceable word.

Appendix E

(Continued)

Word	Origin Information
landscape	Dutch *landschap* meaning "condition of land."
leotard	Jules Leotard, a 19th-century French trapeze artist, created a more comfortable garment to perform in during his act.
lunatic	From the Roman moon goddess, Luna, who supposedly caused people to go mad during the changing phases of the moon.
Mattel	In 1945, Ruth and Elliot Handler, along with Harold "Matt" Matson, started making toys in a Los Angeles garage. The company name was a combination of Matt and Elliot. Years later, Ruth invented "Barbie," named after the Handlers' daughter.
multiply	Latin *multiplicare* meaning "to increase."
muscle	Latin *musculus* meaning "little mouse" from the resemblance of the shape and movement of bicep muscles.
palindrome	Greek *dromos* meaning "running" (also origin of the speedy desert runner, *dromedary*), *palin* means "again."
pedigree	Old French *pie de grue* meaning "crane's foot." A genealogical chart has diagrams indicating who is related to whom, making it evident why speakers of Old French called these charts that looked like webbed feet *pie de grue*.
perimeter	Greek *perimetron* from *peri* meaning "around" and *metron* meaning "to measure."
piggy bank	In the 1400s, household pots and dishes were made of cheap clay called *pygg*. Housewives would store extra coins in *pyggy jars*, and these soon became known as *pygg banks*.
school	Greek *schole* meaning "leisure." Only a man of leisure had time to contemplate, lecture, and discuss. Around 30 B.C. it changed to mean "a place of learning."
serendipity	A made-up word by English author/historian Horace Walpole. In 1754, he wrote a letter claiming he'd coined this word, based on a Persian fairy tale *The Three Princes of Serendip*. He said the heroes "were always making discoveries, by accidents and sagacity, of things they were not in quest of." *Serendip* is a form of *Sarandip*, the old Persian name for Sri Lanka.
starboard	Old English *steorbor*, *steor* meaning "rudder or the steering oar" and *bor* meaning "a side." In the early days, the steering mechanism was on the right-hand side of the ship.
tulip	In the 1500s, Austria's ambassador visited Turkey and was enchanted by the unusual flowers. The Turks' traditional name for the flower was *lale*, but the ambassador's interpreter jokingly called the blossom a *tulbend*, the Turkish word for *turban*, because of its shape. When the ambassador brought home several of these exotic plants, he also brought along its picturesque nickname, *tulbend*, which slightly changed in English.

Copyright material from Mary Jo Fresch (2026), *The Phonics Handbook*, Routledge.

(Continued)

Word	Origin Information
twelve	Proto-Germanic *twa-lif*, a compound of *twa* "two" and *lif* "left." In Old English it became *twelf* meaning "two left over ten."
typhoon	Chinese "tai fung" – *big wind*.
window	When Norse carpenters built homes, they left a hole or eye in the roof to allow smoke to escape. Wind often blew through this hole, and it became known as *vindr auga* meaning "wind eye."
zero	Arabic *sifr* meaning "empty." Middle Latin *zephirum* also meaning "empty."
zipper	B.F. Goodrich company decided to give their 1925 invention a more interesting name than "slide fastener." With the development of the rubber-coated boot, the inventors found a way to describe the speed and sound of this new invention with this word.

Copyright material from Mary Jo Fresch (2026), *The Phonics Handbook*, Routledge.

Appendix F: Application Routines

Routine	Description	Side Work	Small Group	Large Group	Differentiation
Build It	Phonic patterns and additional letter cards are provided to encourage students to build words around the pattern.	Place index cards with patterns and additional letter cards in location for students to work independently to build words.	Meet at small table and show patterns and additional letter cards to students to work together to build words.	Meet at large group area and show patterns and additional letter cards to students to work together to build words.	For more support, provide only letter cards that will build words with the focused pattern. To challenge, include letters that may not make real words.
Find It	Use any text to hunt for focused pattern.	Designate texts students should use to hunt for focused pattern.	Meet at small table, providing texts the group can confidently read to hunt for focused pattern.	Meet at large group area displaying a text large enough that the group can confidently read to hunt for focused pattern.	For more support, use text students can read at 90–100% accuracy, provide the pattern on index cards to assist in visual comparison. To challenge, provide a more complex text and ask students to think of words related to the ones found.

Copyright material from Mary Jo Fresch (2026), *The Phonics Handbook*, Routledge.

(Continued)

Routine	Description	Side Work	Small Group	Large Group	Differentiation
Sort It	Words are provided to compare and contrast to discover phonic patterns.	Place word cards where students can independently work to sort by phonic patterns.	Meet at small table, showing students word cards. Show key words and have students work together to sort by categories.	Meet at large group area showing students word cards. Show key words and have students suggest how to sort by categories.	For more support, provide key words and fewer words to sort. To challenge, do not provide key words and have students sort more difficult words with the pattern.
Remember It	Word cards are matched in this memory game (face down cards are drawn two at time, reading each aloud). If cards drawn do not match, they are turned back over.	Place the word cards where students can lay them out, face down, and play independently or with other students.	Meet at small table, placing the twelve word cards face down. Students take turns flipping cards to make matches, reading aloud each word card.	Meet at large group area showing the twelve word cards face down. Students take turns flipping cards to make matches, reading aloud each word card.	For more support, position six cards face up and six cards face down. The students try to match, reading each card aloud. For challenge, choose more difficult patterns.
Match It	Students match word cards to phonic sound cards.	Place word and phonic sound cards where students can lay them out and match them independently or with other students.	Meet at small table, placing word and phonic sound cards where students can see them. Work together to match the word cards to their phonic sound cards. Ask for additional words to fit the phonic sound pattern.	Meet at large group area, placing word and phonic sound cards where students can see them. Work together to match the word cards to their phonic sound cards. Ask for additional words to fit the phonic sound pattern.	For more support, use fewer phonic sound cards and more word cards that match. To challenge students, give them more difficult word/phonic sound matches. Ask them to give additional words for each sound pattern.

Appendix F

(Continued)

Routine	Description	Side Work	Small Group	Large Group	Differentiation
Unscramble It	Words containing phonic sound patterns students know are cut apart and the letters scrambled. Students work to reassemble each word.	Provide the list of words that have been cut apart, using individual consonants but retaining the phonic sound pattern as one letter card. Students should study the list and unscramble the letters to create the word.	At the small table, gather students and show them a list of words, the individual consonants, and the phonic sound patterns. Ask them to work together to unscramble the letters to reassemble the words on the list.	Meet at large group area. Show students a list of words, the individual consonants, and the phonic sound patterns. Ask them to work together to unscramble the letters to reassemble the words on the list.	For more support, keep the consonant digraphs/blends together to reduce the number of letters needed to reassemble the words. To challenge students, use the same phonics patterns that appear in multisyllabic words.

Bibliography

Adams, Marilyn J. 1990. *Beginning to Read: Thinking and Learning about Print*. Cambridge, MA: MIT Press.

Ash, Sarah L., and Patti H. Clayton. 2009. "Generating, Deepening, and Documenting Learning: The Power of Reflection in Applied Learning." *Journal of Applied Learning in Higher Education, 1*: 25–48.

Bishop, Margaret M. 1986. *The ABC's and All Their Tricks*. Fenton, MI: Mott Media.

Brady, Timothy F., Talia Konkle, George Alvarez, and Aude Oliva. 2008. "Visual Long-Term Memory Has a Massive Storage Capacity for Object Details." *Proceedings of the National Academy of Sciences of the United States of America, 105*(38): 14325–14329.

Bryson, Bill. 1990. *The Mother Tongue: English and How It Got That Way*. New York: William Morrow.

Bryson, Bill. 2013. *Made in America: An Informal History of the English Language in the United States*. New York: William Morrow.

Chall, Jeanne S. 1967. *Learning to Read: The Great Debate*. New York: McGraw-Hill.

Clymer, Theodore. 1963/1996. "The Utility of Phonic Generalizations in the Primary Grades." *The Reading Teacher, 16/50*: 252–258/182–185.

Crystal, David. 2012. *Spell It Out: The Curious, Enthralling, and Extraordinary Story of English Spelling*. New York: St. Martin's Press.

Cunningham, Patricia M. 2009. *Phonics They Use: Words for Reading and Writing*. Boston: Pearson.

Cunningham, Patricia M., and James W. Cunningham. 2002. "What We Know about How to Teach Phonics." In *What Research Has to Say about Reading Instruction* (3rd ed.), edited by Alan E. Farstrup and S. Jay Samuels, 87–109. Newark, DE. International Literacy Association. www.learner.org/wp-content/uploads/2019/02/How-To-Teach-Phonics-HowToTeachPhonics_1.pdf

Diliberto, Jennifer A., John R. Beattie, Claudia P. Flowers, and Robert F. Algozzine. 2008. "Effects of Teaching Syllable Skills Instruction on Reading Achievement in Struggling Middle School Readers." *Literacy Research and Instruction, 48*(1): 14–27. https://doi.org/10.1080/19388070802226253

Ehri, Linnea C. 2014. "Orthographic Mapping in the Acquisition of Sight Word Reading, Spelling Memory, and Vocabulary Learning." *Scientific Studies of Reading, 18*(1): 5–21.

Eide, Denise. 2012. *Uncovering the Logic of English: A Common-sense Approach to Reading, Spelling and Literacy*. Rochester, MN: Logic of English, Inc.

Erbeli, Florina, Marianne Rice, Ying Xu, Megan E. Bishop, and J. Marc Goodrich. 2024. "A Meta-Analysis on the Optimal Cumulative Dosage of Early Phonemic Awareness Instruction." *Scientific Studies of Reading*, *28*(4): 345–370. https://doi.org/10.1080/10888438.2024.2309386

Flesch, Rudolph. 1955. *Why Johnny Can't Read and What You Can Do about It*. New York: Harper & Row.

Fox Searchlight Pictures. 2005. *Bee Season*.

Fresch, Mary Jo. 2000. "What We Learned from Josh: Sorting Out Word Sorting." *Language Arts*, *77*(2) (January): 232–240.

Fresch, Mary Jo, and David L. Harrison. 2020. *Empowering Students' Knowledge of Vocabulary: Learning How Language Works, Grades 3–5*. Champaign, IL: National Council of Teachers of English.

Fresch, Mary Jo, and Aileen Wheaton. 1997. "Sort, Search, and Discover: Spelling in the Child-centered Classroom." *The Reading Teacher*, *51*(1): 20–31.

Fresch, Mary Jo, and Aileen Wheaton. 2002. *Teaching and Assessing Spelling: A Practical Approach That Strikes the Balance between Whole-Group and Individualized Instruction*. Amazon Books.

Fresch, Mary Jo, and Aileen Wheaton. 2019. *The Spelling List and Word Study Resource Book: Organized Spelling Lists, Greek and Latin Roots, Word Histories, and other Resources for Dynamic Spelling and Vocabulary Instruction*. Amazon Books.

Fry, Edward. 1998. "The Most Common Phonograms." *The Reading Teacher*, *51*(7): 620–622.

Fry, Edward Bernard. 1964. *A Frequency Approach to Phonics*. Rutgers University Press.

Gates, Arthur Irving. 1935. *Gates Reading Vocabulary for the Primary Grades*. Columbia University: Teachers College.

Goodman, Kenneth. 1986. "Whole-Language Research: Foundations and Development." *The Elementary School Journal*, *90*(20): 207–221.

Goswami, Usha. 1991. "Learning about Spelling Sequences: The Role of Onsets and Rimes in Analogies in Reading." *Child Development*, *62*(5): 1110–1123. https://doi.org/10.2307/1131156

Goswami, Usha. 2000. "Phonological and Lexical Processes." In *Handbook of Reading Research Volume III*, edited by Michael L. Kamil, Peter B. Mosenthal, P. David Pearson, and Rebecca Barr, 251–267. New York: Routledge.

Gray, William S., and May Hill Arbuthnot. 1946. *Fun with Dick and Jane*. Chicago: Scott Foresman and Company.

Hanna, Paul, Jean Hanna, Richard Hodges, and Edwin Rudorf, Jr. 1966. *Phoneme-grapheme Correspondences as Cues to Spelling Improvement*. Washington, DC: U.S. Office of Education.

Harrison, David L., Timothy V. Rasinski, and Mary Jo Fresch. 2022a. *Partner Poems & Word Ladders for Building Foundational Literacy Skills, Grades K-2*. New York: Scholastic.

Harrison, David L., Timothy V. Rasinski, and Mary Jo Fresch. 2022b. *Partner Poems & Word Ladders for Building Foundational Literacy Skills, Grades 1–3*. New York: Scholastic.

International Literacy Association. 2025. "Literacy Glossary." www.literacyworldwide.org/get-resources/literacy-glossary

Bibliography

Jacobson, Julie, Diane Lapp, and James Flood. 2007. "A Seven-step Instructional Plan for Teaching English-language Learners to Comprehend and Use Homonyms, Homophones, and Homographs." *Journal of Adolescent & Adult Literacy, 51I* (2): 98–111. https://doi.org/10.1598/JAAL.51.2.2

Johnston, Francine. 2001. "The Utility of Phonic Generalizations: Let's Take another Look at Clymer's Conclusions." *The Reading Teacher, 55*(2): 132–143. www.jstor.org/stable/20197636

Joshi, R. Malatesha, Rebecca Treiman, Suzanne Carreker, and Louise C. Moats. Winter 2008–2009. "How Words Cast Their Spell: Spelling is an Integral Part of Learning the Language, Not a Matter of Memorization." *American Educator*. www.aft.org/sites/default/files/joshi.pdf

Kress, Jacqueline E., and Edward B. Fry. 2015. *The Reading Teacher's Book of Lists* (6th ed.). San Francisco, CA: Jossey-Bass.

Martin, Peter. "The Philosophy behind the First American Dictionary." *The Atlantic*, May 28, 2019. www.theatlantic.com/entertainment/archive/2019/05/dictionary-wars-peter-martin-excerpt/588586/

McGuffey, William Holmes. 1836. *McGuffey Readers* (a six volume series). Cincinnati, OH: Truman and Smith.

Melby-Lervåg, Monica, Solvieg-Alma Halaas Lyster, and Charles Hulme. 2012. "Phonological Skills and Their Role in Learning to Read: A Meta-analytic Review." *Psychological Bulletin, 138*(2): 322–352.

Merriam-Webster Dictionary. 2024. www.merriam-webster.com

Moats, Louisa Cook. 2000. *Speech to Print: Language Essentials for Teachers*. Baltimore, MD: Paul H. Brookes Publishing Co.

National Reading Panel. 2000. *Report of the National Reading Panel: Teaching Children to Read: An Evidence-Based Assessment of the Scientific Research Literature on Reading and Its Implications for Reading Instruction: Reports of the Subgroups*. Eunice Kennedy Shriver National Institute of Child Health and Human Development, National Institutes of Health. www.nichd.nih.gov/sites/default/files/publications/pubs/nrp/Documents/report.pdf

Okrent, Arika. 2021. *Highly Irregular: Why Tough, Through, and Dough Don't Rhyme – and Other Oddities of the English Language*. Illustrated by Sean O'Neill. New York: Oxford University Press.

Pearson, P. David, and Margaret C. Gallagher. 1983. "The Instruction of Reading Comprehension." *Contemporary Educational Psychology, 8*: 317–344.

Perfetti, Charles A. 1986. "Continuities in Reading Acquisition, Reading Skill and Reading Disability." *RASE, 7*(1): 11–21.

Piasta, Shayne B. 2014. "Moving to Assessment-Guided Differentiated Instruction to Support Young Children's Alphabet Knowledge." *The Reading Teacher, 68*(3): 202–211. https://doi.org/10.1002/trtr.1316moa

Reading Rockets. 2025. *Word Hunts*. Washington, DC: WETA. www.readingrockets.org/classroom/classroom-strategies/word-hunts

Rehfeld, David M., Marie Kirkpatrick, Nicole O'Guinn, and Rachel Renbarger. 2022. "A Meta-Analysis of Phonemic Awareness Instruction Provided to Children Suspected of Having a Reading Disability". *Language, Speech, and Hearing Services in Schools, 53*(4): 1177–1201. https://doi.org/10.1044/2022_LSHSS-21-00160.

Rycik, Mary T., and James A. Rycik. 2007. *Phonics and Word Identification: Instruction and Intervention, K-8*. Upper Saddle River, NJ: Pearson.

Seidenberg, Mark. 2017. *Language at the Speed of Sight: How We Read, Why So Many Can't, and What Can Be Done about It*. New York: Basic Books.

Spinelli, Jerry. 1990. *Manic Magee*. New York: Scholastic.

Stanback, Margaret L. 1992. "Syllable and Rime Patterns for Teaching Reading: Analysis of a Frequency-based Vocabulary of 17,602 Words." *Annals of Dyslexia, 42*: 196–221.

Thorndike, Edward L., and Irving Lorge. 1944. *The Teacher's Word Book of 30,000 Words*. New York: Bureau of Publications, Teachers College, Columbia University.

Willingham, Daniel T. 2009. Why Don't Students Like School? A Cognitive Scientist Answers Questions about How the Mind Works and What It Means for the Classroom. San Francisco, CA: Wiley.

Wright, Ernest Vincent. 1939. *Gadsby: A Story of over 50,000 Words Without Using the Letter "E"*. Los Angeles: Wetzel Publishing.

Wylie, Richard E., and Donald D. Durrell. 1970. "Teaching Vowels through Phonograms." *Elementary English, 47*: 787–791.

Yidan Prize. 2024. "Uncovering the Roots and Rhythms of Language Learning." https://yidanprize.org/global-community/laureates/usha-goswami/

Index

-*able*: adding, rules 80–82; Build It, usage 88
acronyms 86
Adams, Marilyn 7, 58
affixes (syllable types) 72
affricates, articulation 26, 91
analogy phonics 7
analytic phonics 7
anchor words, usage 43, 47
anticipated misunderstanding 25, 27, 36, 44, 49, 51, 84
antonyms 86
application routines 11; list 107–109; usage 38–39
articulations: examination 27; types 26–27
automaticity, development 65
awareness, meaning 4

base cards, usage 88
base words: -*able*, adding 81; -ing, adding 16–17
Bee Season (Naumann) 85
B(rain), E(ars), E(yes) (B.E.E.), student usage 27, 36, 44, 84
Beginning to Read: Thinking and Learning about Print (Adams) 7
Bishop, Margaret 53
Bishop, Megan 4
blending 1, 5
blends 23; consonant blends 35–37
Build It 13–14; differentiation 14; -*ible* 88; large group, usage 13; rimes 65–66; routine, example 13–14; side work, usage 13; small group, usage 13; usage 11, 13–14, 107; vowel patterns 54

Chall, Jeanne 6
ch sound, Remember It (usage) 39
closed sort, offering 15

closed syllables 72, 101; Sort It, usage 77
Clymer, Theodore 45, 46, 58
cognitive clarity 12, 15, 16
collection sheet, usage 15–16
compound words: Remember It, usage 77; syllabic division 72
consistency rules 46
consonant blends 35–37; end of word usage 36–37; rimes, addition 59
consonant digraphs 32–34; rimes, addition 59; syllable rule 72
consonant -*le*: syllable 74–75; usage, rule 102
consonants 23; air flow, blocking 24; alphabetic list 29–32; articulation 26–27, 91–92; clusters 35; division 72; dropping/doubling, suffix additions (rules) 82–83; generalizations 93–96; importance 24; letters, sounds (retention) 35; silent consonant patterns 37–38; unvoiced initial consonants 25; voiced initial consonants 25; vowel combination, silent *e* 101
consonant sounds 23–32; learning 80; list 93–96; pairing 25; pronunciation, variation (consideration) 27; single-letter representation 24; unvoiced sounds 25; voiced sounds 25
consonant-vowel-consonant (CVC) 44; words, encounter 45
content book, usage 76
content texts, usage 14
Crystal, David 32, 37
Cunningham, Patricia/James 12

decodable books, usage 8
decoding: instruction, phonogram usage (advantage) 58; letter-by-letter decoding 70; manageability 71

115

digraphs 23, 41, 52–53; consonant digraphs 32–34; sounds 14; vowel digraphs 52
Diliberto, Jennifer 69–70
diphthongs 41, 51; rule 101; vowel team, combination 74
doubled/dropped *e*, Find It (usage) 88
Durrell, Donald 43, 48
dyslexic students, syllable instruction 72

Ehri, Linea 18
Eide, Denise 71
embedded phonics 8
ending phonograms, focus 58
ends of words, consonant blends (usage) 36–37
English language: alphabet/sounds, one-to-one match (absence) 3; code 3–5; command, development 2–3; learning 1; statistics 2–3; structure, understanding 29
eponyms 2, 86–87
Erbeli, Florina 4
etymology. *see* word origins: examination 29, 37
executive functions 6

final-*e* generalizations, teachers (usage) 46
final *y*, application routine (usage) 53
Find It 14–15; differentiation 15; doubled consonant/dropped *e* 88; large group, usage 14–15; open syllables 76–77; routine, example 14–15; small group, usage 14; soft *g* sound 38; usage 11, 107
Flesch, Rudolph 6
free reading, selections 14
fricatives, articulation 26, 91
Fresch, Mary Jo 65
Fry, Edward 35
Fun with Dick and Jane (Gray/Arbuthnot) 6

Gadsby: A Story of Over 50,000 Words Without Using the Letter "E" (Wright) 49
Gallagher, Margaret 12
Gates Reading Vocabulary for the Primary Grades 45
generalizations: consideration 45; development 16; utility percentage 45; writing 15–16
glides, articulation 27, 92
gliding sound, creation 51
Goodman, Ken 7
Goodrich, J. Marc 4

Google images, usage (free resource) 54
Goswami, Usha 58–59
graphemes 3
Great Vowel Shift 34, 63
Greek roots, usage 6
Grimm, Jacob 85

Hanna, Jean 28, 53
Hanna, Paul 28, 53
heteronyms 70, 84
high-frequency phonograms 58
Hodges, Richard 28, 53
homographs 84
homonyms 79, 83–84
homophones 83–84
Hulme, Charles 4

I am, who is 85
-*ible*: adding, rules 80–82; Build It, usage 88
independence (building), familiarity (usage) 12
instruction sheet, providing 13

Jespersen, Otto 63
Johnston, Francine 46

key words, establishment 16
Kirkpatrick, Marie 4

large group: Build It, usage 13; Find It, usage 14–15; Match It, usage 19; Remember It, usage 18; Sort It, usage 16–17; Unscramble It, usage 20–21
Latin origin, impact 82
Latin roots, usage 6
-le, -el, -al generalizations 75–76
Learning to Read: The Great Debate (Chall) 6
letter-by-letter decoding 70
letter cards, access 13
letter/sound relationship, knowledge (demonstration) 14
letters, uppercase/lowercase 3
lipogram 49
liquids, articulation 26, 92
listening task 69
listening vocabulary 5
literacy development, consonants (writing) 25
loan words, usage 28

Index

long *a* rimes 62; Match It, usage 66
long *a* sounds, spellings 47
long *e* rimes 63
long *e* sounds, spellings 47–48
long *i* rimes 63
long *i* sounds, spellings 48
long *o* rimes 64
long *o* sounds, spellings 48
long *u* rimes 64
long *u* sounds, spellings 48–49
long vowels 41; vowel-consonant-*e* (VC*e*) pattern 46
long vowel sounds 44–49; confusion 45; patterns 54; short vowel sounds, distinction 42; spellings, list 47–49
Lorge, Irving 28
Lyster, Solvieg-Alma 4

majuscule 3
Match It 18–20; activity 103; differentiation 19–20; large group, usage 19; long *a* rimes 66; *R*-controlled vowel sounds 54; routine, example 19–20; short *a* rimes 66; side work, usage 19; small group, usage 19; usage 11, 108
McGuffey, William 6
Melby-Lervåg, Monica 4
mental task, proficiency 12
Middle English, shift 63
Middle English words 33
minuscule 3
Moats, Louisa Cook 26, 58–59, 71
Modern English, shift 63
morphemes 18
multisyllabic words: patterns, appearance 21; rimes, appearance 57
multi-syllabic words, breaking 70
multisyllabic words, usage (analysis) 28

nasals, articulation 26, 92
nonconformers 45
Normans, impact 28
nyms 86

O'Guinn, Nicole 4
Old English words 33
Old Norse words 52–53
Old Saxon words 52

onset cards, distribution 66
onsets 57; remembrance/usage, ease 58
open sort, offering 15
open syllables 73, 101; Find It, usage 76–77
orthographic mapping 5; sounds/letters, connection importance 18

pattern recognition, search 58–59
pattern words, experience (increase) 17
Pearson, David 12
personal free reading text, usage 14
phonemes 3, 18
phonemic awareness 4
phonic element, finding 14
phonic pattern: letters, addition 13; word hunting 14; writing, 15
phonics: definition 3; fundaments, knowledge (importance) 2; ILA definition 4; instruction 5–6; instruction, history 6–7; knowledge, security (increase) 69; rules, considerations 45; synthetic programs, appearance 6–7; teaching, approaches 7–8; teaching order, issues 35; types 7–8; usage 5
phonic sounds 19; cards, word cards (matching) 18; patterns 20; word count/study 53
phonograms: attention 57; ending phonograms, focus 58; high-frequency phonograms 58; letter-sound relationship 57; list (Wylie/Durrell) **58**
Pixabay, usage (free resource) 54
plosives (stops), articulation 26, 91
prefixes, usage 6
print chunks, recognition 71
printed texts, sleeve protectors (usage) 14
process: scaffolding 12; verbalizing 12

QWERTY 28

R-controlled vowel sounds 41, 49–51; Match It, usage 54; rule 101
R-controlled vowels, syllable 74
readers, skills development (assistance) 2
reading: comprehension, improvement 70; failure, risk 70; programs, rules (examination) 45; skills, improvement 69–70
Rehfeld, David 4
Remember It 17–18; *ch* sound, examination 39; compound words 77; differentiation 18; large

group, usage 18; routine, example 17–18; side work, usage 17–18; small group usage 18; usage 11, 108; word origins 87–88
Renbarger, Rachel 4
Report of the National Reading Panel 7
resources for word lists 45
retronyms 87
rhythm, impact 58–59
Rice, Marianne 4
rime family work 43
rimes 57; adding 59; application routines 65–66; Build It, usage 65–66; cards, usage 65–66; chunks, impact 70; definition 57; identification/grouping 59–64; instruction, importance 58–59; Unscramble It, usage 66; usage/remembrances, ease 58
root cards, usage 88
root words, -*ible* (adding) 81
routines: introducing 12; usage 13
Rudorf, Edwin 28
Rycik, Mary/James 71

schwa 41, 51–52; commonness 52
segmenting 5
Seidenberg, Mark 8
self-confidence, building 12
Sholes, Christopher Latham 28
short *a* rimes 60; Match It, usage 66
short *a* sounds 43
short *e* rimes 60
short *e* sounds 43
short *i* rimes 61
short *i* sounds 44
short *o* rimes 61
short *o* sounds 44
short-term memories 39
short *u* rimes 62
short *u* sounds 44
short vowels 41; -*ing* suffix, wall (creation) 82; representation, vowel team (usage) 63; teaching order 43
short vowel sounds 42–44; long vowel sounds, distinction 42
side practice, routines (applicability) 12
side work: Build It, usage 13; Match It, usage 19; Remember It, usage 17–18; Sort It, usage 16; Unscramble It, usage 20
silent consonant letter/sound correspondences 37

silent consonant patterns 37–38
silent *e* (vowel-consonant rule) 101
silent pairs 23
silent patterns, examination 37
similarities/differences, cognitive clarity 16
single consonants: rimes, addition 59; sounds, examination 24, 27
single letters 23
single vowels, learning ease 43
single words, usage (analysis) 28
singular sound, example 27
small group: Build It, usage 13; Find It, usage 14; Match It, usage 19; Remember It, usage 18; Sort It, usage 16; Unscramble It, usage 20
soft *g* sound, Find It (usage) 38
Sort It 15–17; differentiation 17; large group, usage 16–17; routine, example 15–17; side work, usage 16; small group, usage 16; syllables 77; usage 11, 108
sorts, types (modeling) 15
sound-letter correspondences, predictability 2
sounds: blending 1; consistency/frequency, study 28; gliding sound, creation 51
speech (learning/processing), rhythm (usage) 58–59
spelling: attempts, ears (usage dominance) 36; patterns 28; prediction, sounds (usage) 27
spoken units 18
Stanbuck, Margaret 72–74
sticks (tail strokes) 75
sticky notes, usage 54
stops (plosives), articulation 26, 91
structural analysis 80
suffix cards, usage 88
suffixes, adding 16, 80; consonant dropping/doubling, rules 82–83
suffixes, usage 6
syllables 18, 69; "big picture" rules 72; description, word matching (exercise) 71; direct instruction 70; importance, reasons 69–70; rules 102; teaching 70–71; vowel sounds 72
syllable types 71–76, 101; usage 70–71
synonyms 87
synthetic phonics 8
systematic phonics instruction, importance 18
systematic relationship, learning 4

tail strokes (sticks) 75; examples 76
target words, reassembly 39

Index

task, cognitive clarity 12
Teacher's Word Book of 30,000 Words (Thorndike/Lorge) 28
teaching opportunity 27
Thorndike, Edward 28
two-syllable words, generalizations 46
"two vowels go walking" rule 46

Unscramble It 20–21; differentiation 21; large group, usage 20–21; rimes 66; routine, example 20–21; side work, usage 20; small group, usage 20; usage 11, 109; *wh* words 39
Unsplash, usage (free resource) 54
unvoiced consonants 25
unvoiced initial consonants 25
utility percentage (generalizations) 45

visual support, providing 15
vocal cords, vibration 25
voiced consonants 25
voiced initial consonants 25
vowel-consonant-*e* (VC*e*) pattern 46
vowel-consonant-silent *e* syllable 73
vowels: consonant combination, silent *e* 101; decoding/encoding problems 42; digraphs 52; generalizations 46, 47, 97–99; long vowels 41; patterns, Build It (usage) 54; rules, dependability (absence) 58; short vowels 41; voicing 41
vowel sounds: learning 80; list 97–99; pattern 21; *R*-controlled vowel sounds 49–51, types 41–42
vowel team: diphthong, combination syllable 74; rule 101
vowel team, usage 63

Webster, Daniel 50
whole class activity 66
whole group lessons, class gathering 14–15, 16, 18
Whole Language: appearance 7; methods 7
whole phonograms, learning (ease) 43
wh words, Unscramble It (usage) 39
Why Johnny Can't Read and What You Can Do About It (Flesch) 6
Willingham, Daniel 12
word cards: creation 77; matching 17; phonic elements, presence 19; phonic sound cards, matching 18; usage 15
word list, studying 20
word origins (etymology) 85–86; honoring 29; list 103–106; Remember It, usage 87–88
words: attack, improvement 70; categories, creation 15; chunks, usage 59; families 57; identification, improvement 70; Latin origin, impact 82; oddities, percentage 2–3; orthographic mapping, expansion 43; pairs, consonant doubling/dropping 82; pronunciation, change 80; reading/writing, proficiency (increase) 71; recognition, automaticity (development) 65; tracking 85
words, decoding: rules, usage/examination 45; syllable types, usage 69–70
word study activity 14
Wright, Ernest Vincent 49
written units, connection (formation) 18
Wylie, Richard 43, 58

Xu, Ying 4

For Product Safety Concerns and Information please contact our EU
representative GPSR@taylorandfrancis.com
Taylor & Francis Verlag GmbH, Kaufingerstraße 24, 80331 München, Germany

www.ingramcontent.com/pod-product-compliance
Lightning Source LLC
Chambersburg PA
CBHW080925300426
44115CB00018B/2945